END OF THE GOOD LIFE

*How the Financial Crisis Threatens a Lost Generation—
and What We Can Do About It*

RIVA FROYMOVICH

HARPER ● PERENNIAL

NEW YORK ● LONDON ● TORONTO ● SYDNEY ● NEW DELHI ● AUCKLAND

HARPER ● PERENNIAL

HarperCollins books may be purchased for educational, business, or sales promotional use. For information please e-mail the Special Market Department at SPsales@harpercollins.com.

FIRST EDITION

Designed by Fritz Metsch

Library of Congress Cataloging-in-Publication Data is available upon request.

ISBN 978-0-06-221784-4

13 14 15 16 17   OV/RRD   10 9 8 7 6 5 4 3 2 1

For my parents: Thank you.
And in honor of your parents, and the parents before that.
For our future, together, Lee.

CONTENTS

End of The Good Life

Prologue: The American Dream

There was a time when the American Dream was not an illusion.

In 1981, a young couple named Joseph and Esfira took a risk and headed to America from the former Soviet Union. He was 31 years old; she was 28. They didn't know the language of their new country or where they would live. They just knew they wanted to do better for themselves, and the United States was the place to do that.

Joseph had grown up in a two-room basement apartment in Chernivtsi, a small city in today's southwest Ukraine. He lived with his parents and four siblings in a space that had previously housed barnyard animals. The apartment shared a dirt courtyard and an outhouse with two other small apartment buildings. Because it sat at the bottom of a steep unpaved road, whenever it rained, muddy water seeped through the single window and the dungeon-like space flooded.

Joseph's parents earned a meager living as tailors and sometimes asked him to beg neighbors for help. When it came time to enroll in middle school, his parents sent him off to a government-funded boarding school because they couldn't afford to feed all their children. On the weekends, when he returned home, Joseph would watch his mother, Ester, make a three-course meal out of potatoes. He often woke up in the middle of night to the sound of his father, Shalom, hunched over a sewing machine, making coats to sell on the black market to earn extra cash to support the family. For no reason except his own imagination, Joseph dreamed he could have more.

As a teenager and young adult, Joseph grew increasingly determined to shape his future. He became a gymnast and grew disciplined. He set his sights on becoming the first person in his family to go to college—and he did.

He studied at night toward a master's degree in physics and engineering from Chernivtsi National University while working at a local factory during the day. Before graduating, he met and married Esfira, who went on to receive her own advanced degree in mathematics from the same school. They moved in with her parents, sharing a one-bedroom apartment on the top floor of a five-story walk-up building constructed during the Khrushchev era in the 1960s. When they welcomed their first child into the world, the apartment then had to fit five. Esfira and Joseph wanted to give their new daughter more than communal living and potato dinners. So, like many before them, they packed their few possessions and headed to a land of opportunity: America.

They rented the ground-floor apartment of a two-family house in Staten Island, New York, with the help of the New York Association for New Americans (NYANA), an agency that was established in 1949 to help settle survivors of the Holocaust and that went on to serve refugees from across the world. In the United States, Joseph and Esfira's education opened the way for careers that gave them opportunities to build their lives, so they no longer had to live hand to mouth.

To boost Esfira's math background, NYANA set her up with English-language and bookkeeping courses to prepare her for job interviews. Once she was ready to apply for positions, NYANA sent out her resume, and the main branch of Harlem Savings Bank in Manhattan, later renamed Apple Bank for Savings, called Esfira in for a meeting. It was difficult for her to answer their questions, and as she walked home from the train station following the interview, Esfira was nervous and realized that she didn't even fully understand the responsibilities of the job. But Joseph and their daughter were waiting for her in the doorway before she even arrived back at the apartment. "They called! You got it," Joseph shouted. Her starting salary was $9,000 per year. She sobbed with happiness. Esfira soon learned she would be an accounting clerk, responsible for inputting monthly mortgage payments, depositing checks, and updating account records—the type of work that computers mostly handle independently today. About thirty years later, in 2010, Esfira was earning more than ten times as much at another company, just before she was laid off and her job was outsourced to India.

To find his first job, Joseph visited the New York Public Library in Manhattan. It took him three days to search through books in the grand Beaux-Arts landmark on Fifth Avenue to figure out the English terminology for his profession—nondestructive testing—so he could explain the kind of job he wanted to his caseworker at NYANA, Mrs. Nobel. She was a warm and competent 80-something woman with a sincere desire to help, someone whom Joseph often fondly remembers. She set up two interviews for Joseph. At first it was too difficult for him to communicate with the interviewer. His English was still poor, and he was rejected. Joseph had better luck on his second interview, at Lucius Pitkin Inc. in lower Manhattan, and secured his first job in America as an engineer. He was paid $14,000 per year. "I was very happy. Everybody else was getting much more money, but I didn't know. When I did find out, I was still very happy," he said.

Joseph and Esfira scraped and saved for two years to buy their first house, a space big enough to comfortably raise their now two children. It had three bedrooms, two floors, a yard, and a pool. They put down $10,000 to make the purchase and took out a $64,000 thirty-year loan from the State of New York Mortgage Agency (SONYMA). Their basement was soon filled with toys and electronic gadgets, and a new burgundy Buick was parked in their driveway.

"Two years after being in this country, and I was able to purchase a house and give birth to my second child. In Russia, I wasn't making enough money my whole life to do that. My mother saved her whole life for my wedding, and she still didn't have enough," said Esfira.

Within a couple more years, they took their next risk: Joseph started his own small engineering business that tested the integrity of metals in items such as air-conditioning units and train tracks. It was a niche business, and it thrived. Esfira also advanced, moving up the corporate ladder as a computer analyst.

Then the couple did what Americans are supposed to do: they traded up. They sold their house and built a bigger home in a nicer neighborhood. They invested in stocks and bonds for their retirement, as American television and convention told them. They put money into savings accounts for their children's future. They traveled to Caribbean islands and Europe. They ate meat or fish almost every day.

They sent their kids to sleepaway camp and enrolled them in piano lessons, dance studios, and painting classes.

In less than ten years, Joseph and Esfira managed to move into the middle class. They were able to give their children more than Shalom or Ester ever could have imagined. They achieved the American Dream.

Joseph and Esfira are my parents, and their story of economic mobility is becoming more and more difficult to achieve for young people today. In a sign of the changing times, the organization that helped them settle down in the United States, NYANA, was shut down in 2008, after almost sixty years of service, in large part because it was no longer able to raise the funds needed to assist newcomers.[1]

Introduction: End of The Good Life

He had come a long way to this blue lawn, and his dream must have seemed so close that he could hardly fail to grasp it. He did not know that it was already behind him, somewhere back in that vast obscurity beyond the city, where the dark fields of the republic rolled on under the night.

—F. Scott Fitzgerald, *The Great Gatsby*

It will sound to you like some dystopian universe, but everyone should have seen this coming. Indeed, many leaders have just ignored it.

From tax changes to national spending priorities to labor laws, economic policies progressively implemented since my parents settled in America in the 1980s have systematically cut off opportunities for young adults to move up the economic ladder. But the financial crisis that started in 2007 and plummeted the country into the Great Recession has made that goal even harder to reach. The economic turmoil has become the biggest threat to individual prosperity and the global economy since the Great Depression in the 1930s. It has exposed vulnerabilities in the economy long ignored, and magnified them, creating extraordinary hurdles for this nation's future.

As a result, Generation Y, roughly defined as those born between 1976 and 2000, can expect lower wages and less job security as they compete with peers in faster-growing economies such as China's and Brazil's. They can expect a higher cost of living as the prices of energy and food remain near the highest levels in history. These young workers will have to get by with fewer benefits, including health care and pensions, since most governments in the developed world are severely in debt. In fact, as they struggle to rebalance bloated budgets, leaders will probably deem much federal social support unsustainable and will also allow companies to reduce benefits for the sake of desperately needed profits. Generation Y will likely have to pay higher taxes to make up for the large government debts and to support an unprecedented aging of the population in the "richest" countries in the world. So far, that's less pay and job security, and less federal support despite those higher taxes. But many will feel lucky to have a job at all. Unemployment is expected to remain relatively high well into the future after thousands of jobs were wiped away by the financial crisis. Their return would require large amounts of federal stimulus—money that the government has so far been unwilling to commit, given the nation's high debt. As a result, many in Generation Y will accept jobs for which they are significantly overqualified, wasting a top-notch education they went into personal debt for, as well as the skills they acquired along the way in unpaid internships. Generation Y will also find it more difficult to take out a mortgage to buy a home, given tougher loan rules. But many won't be able to afford to buy a home anyway. Stock markets will be too volatile for ordinary people to earn a supplementary income through investing—and hedge funds that the little guy just can't compete with will continue to dominate the market. Many young people are already scarred by the financial market instability seen during the crisis, and upset that scandals such as Bernard Madoff's massive Ponzi scheme have led to only limited financial regulatory reforms. All this will leave the Millennial generation with fewer opportunities to save money for its future and higher hurdles for starting a family and transitioning into independence.

This is what we have to look forward to if no real change occurs. An entire generation raised—perhaps with a sense of self-entitlement—to optimistically chase its dreams, believe in the power of hard work, and be confident in America's economic progress, led by examples such as my parents, will have to face a much harsher reality than they ever imagined and find a new way to a stable life. And the phenomenon is not contained to the United States. The impact on Generation Y will be felt across the most developed, industrialized, and advantaged countries in the world.

This marks the End of The Good Life, the end of a certain set of expectations—promised by our parents and governments for decades—for how we should live, what we should value, and what we can achieve. The financial crisis exacerbated accumulating problems in the global economy and revealed the illusion. Its most disappointing and enduring upshot will be the loss of one of modern society's greatest values: the globalized American dream of doing better than the generation before. Instead, Generation Y could be stuck in limbo, never quite becoming the people they hoped to be, and missing out on a fair chance at economic and social mobility. America's most important asset, the skills and economic contributions of its people, will be subverted.

Snapshot of Generation Y and America Today

Millennials are entering adulthood at a period of historically high joblessness, with youth unemployment at nearly record highs and exceeding the rate in the broader population at least two times over. The Great Recession of 2008 and 2009 in the United States saw the largest increase in the youth unemployment rate since government began collecting data in 1948—and it could take another decade before all the lost jobs are recovered.[1] That's young people getting their lives back on track ten years late. Generation Y won't be so young anymore by then. Making matters worse, many of these Millennials carry a staggering amount of debt from financing a top-notch education that is having very little payoff. Outstanding student loans are now greater than both national credit card loans and car loans.[2] Those arrears grow each month someone is out of a job; each month someone is out of a job, the more likely that person will stay out of a job for another month. The cycle is difficult to escape.

As a result, many members of Generation Y are living with parents or other relatives long after they should have moved out, working in unpaid or low-paid jobs just to keep resumes filled with something, agonizing over whether they can afford to have children, and struggling to secure a small-business loan with a reasonable interest rate.

Generation Y in the United States isn't facing a crisis alone. In Spain, half of all young people are out of work. In the United Kingdom, one out of every five young people has no job. Lower or even negative economic growth in several European economies after the crisis will make it that much harder for job numbers and wages to recover, sidelining a generation of young people there. A study by the Office for National Statistics in the United Kingdom confirmed these fears. It showed that college graduates today are having a much tougher time finding work than college graduates in the early 1990s. And those who are charmed enough to find a job are working well below their potential. More than one in every three recent diploma recipients work in a low-skilled job, compared with about one out of every four in 2001. Those low-skilled jobs, which came after three years of university, include postal workers, hotel porters, cleaners, and catering assistants.

Of course, Generation Y is fortunate in many ways compared to generations that came before. But it seems as though all those advantages are going to waste. We are the most educated group of 20-somethings in history, living in the twenty-first century, and we just can't afford to grow up. Now that I'm 28 years old, just like my mother when she moved across the Atlantic Ocean, I fear with good reason that I won't be able to provide as much for my children—or for myself—as my parents did for me. Sadly, this fear is apparent in many of my peers as well.

Already, the anger is boiling over in demonstrations around the globe, as the immediate effects of the crisis start to hint at what's to come, because underemployment and low pay at a young age have knock-on effects on the rest of a person's working life.

There have been Occupy Wall Street protests in New York, *indignados* taking over squares with blankets and picket signs in Spain, and thousands rioting in Greece, armed with gasoline bombs and bottles. Ireland has seen a massive youth outflow, as have southern European nations, including

Portugal. And those are just a few examples of the anxiety seizing young people in places where they are supposed to benefit from an advantaged position in the world.

"The social compact is starting to unravel in many countries. Young people who see no future for themselves feel increasingly disenfranchised," said Angel Gurria, secretary-general of the Organization for Economic Co-operation and Development (OECD), one of the world's largest think tanks.

These countries have hundreds of years of economic, technological, and social developments behind them, but many in Generation Y know they are not just facing a short-term hiccup. Top economists warn that permanent scars could tarnish today's young, affecting earnings potential and financial stability for many years to come—factors that are also tied to happiness and health. When the starting point for a person's salary is historically low, their salary will probably stay relatively low throughout their career, because earnings are unlikely to suddenly jump to make up for the difference. Salary raises usually come in small increments. In the same way, if someone is unemployed for an extended period of time, even after that person finds another job, his or her income will take an indefinite hit. In other words, Generation Y will feel the consequences of beginning their careers during a recession for the rest of their working life.

Generation Y's trauma does not affect young people alone. As growing up—getting a job, moving out, starting one's own family—becomes more difficult for Millennials, baby-boomer parents will have to support their children for longer, even as their savings and wealth have also been struck by the crisis. Moreover, lost opportunities for

Generation Y could eventually hurt overall United States productivity, increase the burden for government support, and damage America's global competitiveness. It could also undercut innovation in the sciences, arts, and technology, especially as the government aims to slash spending to fend off the effects of the crisis and rebalance its budget. Moreover, it could mean Generation Y won't be able to afford to pay back its student loans, a growing threat to the entire economy. That is why what is at stake today is not only the future of a generation. It is nothing less than the cornerstone of America's identity and the country's position as a global leader. Federal Reserve chairman Ben Bernanke—an expert on economic crises and the Great Depression—called it "the worst financial crisis in global history" for good reason.[3]

People know and understand this: it is years after the recession ended, yet confidence indicators, such as the Conference Board's Consumer Confidence Index and Gallup's Economic Confidence Index, remain mired at recessionary levels as economic growth stays anemic. The United States Congressional Budget Office warns that production and employment are likely to stay well below the economy's potential for a number of years. Especially worrying is the growing mismatch, ever since the crisis, between the requirements for available jobs and the skills of job seekers.[4] But rather than tackle this slow recovery in jobs, growth, and confidence head-on, governments worldwide are embarking on new strategies that amplify these effects, ignoring the pain this will cause for today's younger generations.

Economic growth is being further hindered across the globe as the advanced economies focus on cutting their deficits—the difference between government revenues and spending. These governments have relied on their status in the world to borrow beyond their means. Now, fearful of losing the confidence of financial markets, they are intent on reining in spending and increasing revenues—no matter, it seems, the pain it causes citizens. The United States is set to take more aggressive measures in the years ahead, even as the continent-wide drive by governments in Europe to rapidly institute extraordinary cuts to social benefits, wages, and key services has yielded troubling results. The goal of the European Union—a twenty-seven-member economic bloc that stretches from Finland to Malta, Romania to Portugal—was to make the region's economies more competitive in the future. However, most European countries ended up driving themselves into a second recession through a significant and coordinated fiscal tightening. One-fifth of the population 30 years of age and under is unemployed. Meanwhile, 40 percent of those who do have jobs are on temporary contracts, lacking both security and benefits.

While the drive for balancing budgets is rooted in merit—running large deficits is an unsustainable policy—it defies logic in the current context. The world has just experienced its most severe economic shock in more than half a century. Citizens are still struggling after the crisis, and initiatives that will hamper growth for years to come risk a lost generation. History shows this policy doesn't work to reinvigorate economies. Worse still, insiders say that countries have been so consumed by the crisis and fixing national finances that few have carried out the essential reforms they have pledged in order to aid young people and alleviate the effects of budget cuts and tax hikes.

But it's easy for politicians to ignore Generation Y:

today's 20- and early-30-somethings are an underrepresented group of voters in a population dominated by those nearing retirement. We are vulnerable.

The Long View: How We Got Here and What It Means

The view from here is worrying. Aren't things supposed to get better over time, not worse? Wages and national productivity rose for an entire generation after World War II, thanks to government policies that found jobs for millions upon millions of returning veterans, empowered union organizers, protected workers so that they were paid fairly, prohibited discrimination, sought to ensure the safety of consumer products, and then into the 1960s aimed to eliminate poverty altogether with intensive spending programs. From just before the stock market crashed in 1929, when the wage gap between rich and poor reached a record high, the inequality gap declined into the 1950s, and it continued to shrink moderately through the 1970s. Home and car ownership rates rose, education improved, and modern technology offered newfound comforts. This period cemented a bygone ideal in the shadow of the Great Depression: the American dream.

Then everything changed. Over the past thirty years, shifting economic policies in the United States have made it much harder for young people to just get by, let alone do better than those who came before them. Starting in Washington, D.C., and trickling down to the American people, there has been a determined shift in power to a small group of the wealthy. As a result, the income gap began to expand again, culminating today in the collapse of incomes and of hope.

Into the 1980s, the government tried to revive the economy following oil crises and a stock market crash via widespread business and financial deregulation, a drop in the minimum wage, the breakdown of unions, and the privatization of many public services in order to lower the costs to government.[5] This period marked "a significant departure from a five-decade trend toward greater economic and social equality," according to John Schmitt of the Center for Economic and Policy Research, an expert on inequality in the United States labor market.[6] What changed, he said, was the balance of power between workers and their employers.

This shift manifested in tax policies that favored higher-income households and further increased their concentration of wealth, particularly in the latest decade. At the same time, working-class salaries declined as American workers had to compete in a globalized world against cheaper labor and less regulation in Indonesia or China, for example. More United States businesses opened posts in those cheaper emerging market countries, which also reduced the number of jobs available in the United States. In this way, national policies that opened America's workplace to global competition, making companies and their executives richer, ended up hurting a lot of the workforce. Employees were helpless because at the same time the power and influence of labor unions disintegrated. The shift additionally manifested through the decline of government funding for education. One's home address—rich neighborhood versus less rich neighborhood—became the difference between a good and a bad public school education. As a result, the gulf between the academic performance of children from higher-income households and lower-income households continues to increase. Government funding was reduced to higher education too, which meant students who weren't wealthy had to go into debt to finance their future. The combination of all these policies pushed the low and high ends of the income spectrum further and further apart. The impact for Generation Y is clear in the numbers.

The net worth of a typical household headed by an adult under the age of 35 is now 68 percent less than households headed by same-age counterparts in 1984.[7] So, underprivileged young adults are getting locked out of the middle class, and those born into the middle class are now struggling to maintain their lifestyle as they become independent. Indeed, according to the Economic Mobility Project, a third of Americans raised in the middle class now fall out of it as adults.[8] This generational income gap comes alongside a widening gap in America between the rich and everyone else too. The difference between the top and lowest income levels in the United States has now almost caught up to where it was just before the Great Depression, having risen sharply since 2002. That means the richest 1 percent of the United States population now owns more than 20 percent of the nation's income. If you imagine every single dollar bill circulating in the country, the richest Americans have one out of every five in their back pocket. It wasn't always like that. About thirty years earlier, in 1980, the top 1 percent of earners took home just 8 percent of all after-tax income in the United States. That's less than half of what they have today. At the same time as this transformation for the rich has occurred, the middle class and poorer income groups have experienced the exact opposite. The share of national income owned by middle-class earners has shrunk to its lowest level, about 14 percent, while the share of national income going to the bottom fifth of U.S. households has declined from 7 percent in 1979 to 5 percent in 2007.[9] In the past, these lower earners saw more progress. Between 1968 and 1980, economic policies helped this group more than double their income share from 5 percent to 11 percent.[10] But today, nearly half of all Americans are either impoverished or categorically "low-income," and there is a growing class of working poor.[11] Moreover, parental income is more correlated with children's income in the United States than in any other leading economy.[12]

Understanding the evolution of the divide in income levels is important to see the hurdles set for Generation Y as they try to achieve the American dream in the aftermath of the financial crisis, which has made it so much harder for everyone to make economic progress. As Nobel Prize winner and economist Joseph Stiglitz said: "An economy in which most citizens are doing worse year after year—an economy like America's—is not likely to do well over the long haul."[13] However, it is also important because the very existence of a divide ultimately damages the society we live in. According to research by Richard G. Wilkinson, coauthor of *The Spirit Level*, a wide divide between haves and have-nots within a country materially harms the health and stability of communities. Life spans actually shrink. Wilkinson examined a spectrum of developed and rich countries, and discovered that mental illness, homicide, and school dropout rates, among other societal ills, are higher inside more unequal nations. In addition, his research shows that low economic mobility—and its effects—is more prevalent in the United States than anywhere else.

"If Americans want to live the American dream, they should go to Denmark," he says.[14]

However, the concentration of wealth in the hands of few and the damaging effects of the crisis are global phenomena. The average income of the richest 10 percent of the population in the advanced economies combined—including Australia, the United Kingdom, Germany, and Japan—is now about nine times that of the poorest 10 percent. So Generation Y in much of the Western world is facing some of the same hurdles to economic mobility.

This recession has laid bare the problem of another government policy from the last thirty years: building an economy on the immaterial.

The United States thought it could keep up the American dream, with each generation getting richer, in a service economy that stopped investing in infrastructure or supporting manufacturing inside the country. By and large, the United States ceased making tangible things at the same rate as decades before, and it stopped being a place for self-sustaining industries that could back the country's growing debts or shoulder job losses. (In contrast, Germany's strong manufacturing sector made it a beacon of economic strength during even the worst times of the European crisis that began in 2009. It could create jobs and sell products to keep the economy in good condition.) Instead, the United States economy became a place of valuable ideas. In many ways, this is a good thing. The country's culture of innovation has helped make it one of the best countries in the world in which to build a business, supported by laws that require relatively minimal legal paperwork and few expenses to be an entrepreneur compared to other countries. It is a forward-thinking economy where taking risks is highly rewarded.

However, there were also downsides to this decades-long shift that became apparent once the financial crisis struck in 2007. In this environment, where the immaterial—such as banking and information technology—prevailed, the financial sector was allowed to grow out of control. It made money and jobs, and leaders liked that. But it also took dangerous bets that made money seem as worthless as the colorful bills in a Monopoly board game—and it might as well have been, the way everyone was acting. (Interestingly, it was in the years just prior to the crisis that the United States Treasury introduced new colors on traditional greenbacks, which for nearly a hundred years were only green and black, as a security measure.) Banks borrowed lots of money to make these bets, becoming highly leveraged. They created a system where debts are moved from one account or bank to another and then used to fund another bet, expanding and expanding the debts without there ever being anything real to back them up. And everyone is sucked into the banks' game, becoming vulnerable to their mistakes, because banks are such a huge part of our economy. We have been directed to invest our hard-earned savings in stocks and bonds to build a retirement portfolio, ignore the risks that banks take and the fact that returns are not guaranteed. Because home ownership is an immutable value of American life, people have been convinced they can afford a home that they can't, and have been offered loans that make it seem possible. Banks also created financial instruments to trade on the homes' value, since they were already tied to the property through their loans to home buyers. In this way, banks helped to push up the value of homes beyond realistic measures on the promise of what the property could be worth. As a result, now it's not just the banks that are overextended; the average citizen and small business can fall deep into debt too. When trust in all these intangible financial instruments and housing prices sank, it left a gaping hole in the economy. The unwinding of this debt, or deleveraging, as commentators on financial television say, will still take more time.

But the latest crisis wasn't the first incident in recent history when some important lessons could have been learned and implemented, although it was certainly the most dramatic. The lack of banking sector oversight was surprising, given that a miniature version of the financial crisis occurred just ten years earlier due to similar derivative instruments. Like the bankers of today, the hedge fund Long-Term Capital Management also hazardously used high-leverage strategies in the late 1990s, leading to billions of dollars in losses, frozen credit lending, and volatile financial market reactions. In the aftermath, leaders said they would take a deeper look at rules on derivatives and how much a bank can invest beyond the cash that it actually holds. But leaders did not follow through. Banking sector regulations just continued to loosen. Now history is repeating itself. And again, reforms to prevent another serious problem are limited. In closed-door meetings, regulators say it is impossible to prevent another crisis again.

Ultimately, the message for Generation Y has been this: Work harder and longer, receive less, be happy you have work, and don't think about how the boomers totally over-inflated the global economy and deceived you for the thrill of cheap stocks in the 1990s and cheap real estate in the 2000s. Also, ignore the higher and higher taxes that eat up your salary to pay for that aging population and budget fixing, instead of your future, and the fact that economic policies being implemented now to save countries and financial markets will harm your prospects of success. That's really a raw deal, because we didn't make this mess and it shouldn't undo us.

United States president Barack Obama said, "Yes we can." Yes, my immigrant parents could work hard to buy their dream home. And they did. Yes, they could find jobs and stability to raise a family in America and save money. And they did.

But today, *no we can't.*

The status quo for those highlighted in this book, young people who are struggling to make ends meet and attempt to rewrite the future that they were promised, is not fair or right. A lot of them—brave, hopeful and, enterprising—wouldn't say it, but I will: if government doesn't start taking this problem seriously, then we are all screwed.

1

This New American Life: Generation Y and the Great Recession

DR. HIBBERT: To raise the money, we'll need a bond issue.
LISA: But won't that shift a burden to your children?
BART: No, you idiot. We just pay with another bond issue. *(Points to Maggie.)* Let her figure out someone to dump it on.
MAGGIE: *(Looks to her side and sees nobody sitting next to her. She crosses her arms.)*

—**The Simpsons,** Season 19, "E. Pluribus Wiggum"

Shane Patrick has been volunteering at Occupy Wall Street for several months. He sits in its Manhattan office, just a block away from the New York Stock Exchange, hunched over a computer with two Internet browsers running simultaneously.

Occupy is a protest movement that has spread around the world. It has no single message or leader, but channels a growing dissatisfaction with economic inequality and government policies that favor a small and privileged segment of the population. The office is like most in downtown Manhattan: a maze of cubicles bordered by glass-encased offices, gray carpeting, fluorescent lighting. But there are also posters emblazoned with *We The 99 Percent*, a slogan the movement has taken on to highlight how most of the world's wealth is held by just 1 percent of its inhabitants.

When Shane is not responding to emails from media organizations and volunteers anxious to help Occupy, he switches to the other browser for his ongoing job search. He's been looking for work, almost any kind of work, for more than a year. He's 32 years old, has fifteen years of work experience, and becomes more frustrated every day.

Shane grew up as the only child in a working-class family in Queens, New York, and didn't want to rely on his parents after high school, so he moved straight into the job market. He booked concerts for bands and worked on their publicity campaigns. As time went on, he tried his hand in other fields, including social work. He served as a residential counselor in a housing complex for homeless people in and out of psychiatric hospitals. This was before the financial crisis, and finding work came fairly easy. But Shane hit a glass ceiling when it came to wages, because he didn't have a college education. He couldn't advance to a higher position or receive a larger salary. Seeing no alternative, after dabbling part-time for years Shane decided to take the plunge and enroll full-time at City College of New York.

He didn't have enough savings to pay for school. But, like many others, Shane reasoned that a higher-paying job was at the end of the tunnel if he took the risk, applied for loans, and secured a degree.

In August 2008, Shane applied for a small private loan, which he asked his father to cosign, in order to test the waters. He was approved and awarded the sum. Four months later he went back to the same lender, with all the same credentials, and resubmitted an application for a second loan for the next semester of school. He was denied.

"They told me their internal rules were reset," said Shane.

Shane was a victim of horrible timing. In the months since his first loan, financial markets had crashed in the United States.

In September, the United States government was forced to rescue loan behemoths Fannie Mae and Freddie Mac, the country's two largest mortgage finance companies. In the same month, the fourth-largest investment bank in the country, Lehman Brothers, was allowed to fail; it filed for bankruptcy after losing billions of dollars, most of its clients, and the trust of other market participants due to its exposure to the United States housing market. Other institutions also came under pressure on account of their exposure to the collapsing housing market and declining liquidity in the United States money system. Merrill Lynch sold itself to Bank of America, Washington Mutual was seized by the Federal Deposit Insurance Corporation and sold to JPMorgan Chase, and Wachovia was sold to Citigroup. In the following month, legislators agreed on a $700 billion bailout bill, but the effects of the United States crisis had already started seeping into Europe. It became a global economic crisis. In 2008, the Dow Jones Industrial Average had some of its most volatile trading days in the stock index's more than century-long history. But this was only the beginning, and uncertainty in the financial sector transformed into a recession that struck people far away from Wall Street.

Shane's parents argued with him to stay in school and accept their money to pay for his education. He relented, concluding he would be able to pay them back easily once he got a decent job with his college diploma. Shane was able to tap some federal loans and somehow scrape by. But over time it became a strain on his parents. His father's income as a superintendent in an apartment building in Queens couldn't cover all the costs, and they had to dip into their retirement funds to pay for Shane's college.

"My parents were helping me to barely survive with what little they could spare from my father's social security payments and whatever other small amounts that could be spared from their income, which was combined with what little I could get in loans," said Shane. "His social security was coming every month and it went straight to me."

Shane felt guilty, but he did as his parents asked. He graduated at 31 years of age with a degree in history and political science.

Before, Shane had no degree and steady work. Now he has a degree and no job, amid the highest unemployment rate in decades, and is thousands of dollars in debt. He wanted to become a teacher, but Shane hasn't limited his job search. He has also looked for jobs that matched his previous experience in social work and publicity. He scours the Internet for job advertisements daily and asks family and friends to look out for openings, and while he has been called in for a handful of interviews, none of them has yet proven fruitful.

"In hindsight, I had a deluded expectation that having a college degree and this job experience would help me get a job," he said. "There's this whole rhetoric that if you structure your resume a certain way or wear something specific it will help . . . but it's just magical thinking because there are just so many people unemployed," said Shane.

In debt to his father for more than $30,000, he has also accrued about $7,000 in credit card debt and has another

$30,000 in outstanding student loans to private lenders and the government. He keeps deferring the payments, but Shane is worried that he won't be able to do so for much longer.

Shane takes up temporary and part-time work contracts whenever he can to help pay the bills in a Brooklyn apartment he shares with his girlfriend of six years. He recently assisted a New York computer software company, doing work completely unrelated to his academic training or experience, and still relies on his parents for occasional help.

Shane is often removed and introspective. He wanted by now to be in a place in his life where he and his girlfriend could have bought a home. He can't even broach the topic of children.

"I'm perpetually thinking, 'What did I do wrong here?' and reevaluating options, and I'm kind of exhausting every which possible way. . . . This amount of uncertainty at this point in my life leads to an existential crisis. You see people around you . . . and you feel like you're running on a treadmill."

At the Occupy demonstrations, Shane found others who shared his frustration at this new American life. On www .wearethe99percent.tumblr.com, a website that evolved alongside the Occupy movement, hundreds of people have posted their worries, giving voice to an even larger portion of the population.

From a 26-year-old woman on the site: "If I want to go any further in my chosen job field, I need a master's degree, which I can't get without taking out loans. The thought of doing that terrifies me. So many of my friends are struggling with more debt than I am, or can't find jobs despite looking diligently, or are stuck in jobs they hate but can't afford to quit. We were told that going to college was the way to ensure we had bright futures. That taking out loans would be worth it. That if we worked hard and did our part, it would pay off. We did our part—what now?"

The Facts and Figures
of This New American Life

It's little wonder that almost half of American adults between the ages of 18 and 34 believe they may end up worse off than their parents, and 68 percent say it is harder to make ends meet since the recession began.[1]

Members of Generation Y have good reason to be concerned for their future.

The financial crisis ushered in a United States unemployment rate that saw one person out of every ten out of work. But for those between 16 and 24 years of age, nearly one out of every five couldn't find work. Those figures don't even capture the whole story for recent high school and college graduates. Many have dropped out of the job hunt altogether, frustrated with a lack of results. Youth employment has fallen to a more than sixty-year low, with just 54 percent of Americans between 18 and 24 years old in jobs. And then there is underemployment—those who settle for part-time work or temporary contracts, which young people are disproportionately saddled with. These types of posts usually offer no security or benefits and are reserved for newer entrants into the workplace, who have few alternatives in this economic climate and limited work experience—two assets employers sometimes take advantage of. For Generation Y, the impact on income is already clear: 37 percent of United States households led by someone under the age of 35 have a net worth of zero or less than zero.[2] That means more than one-third of Generation Yers trying to be independent after the crisis are failing. They are in debt or just barely getting by.

The longer the unemployment rate remains elevated—and it's expected to stay so for up to another decade—the higher the risk that Millennials will suffer from long-term joblessness, which portends such long-term scars as lower wages, diminished appeal to employers, loss of confidence, and even a shorter life span. In a study of a mixed-age group of Pennsylvania workers who lost their jobs in the 1970s and 1980s, it was the youngest who suffered the biggest impact on life expectancy.[3] Part of the reason may be because they earned less for the rest of their life. If a man spends one year unemployed before the age of 23, ten years later he can expect to earn 23 percent less than someone who was steadily employed. For women, the gap is 16 percent. And for both sexes, the penalty persists into middle age.[4] Workers with large losses in earnings tend to have more job instability and chronic stress associated with lower levels of income and volatility in their lives, imperiling their health and ultimately their life.

Even those young people who have remained employed through the crisis will likely experience reduced wages. About half of American workers between the ages of 18 and 34 say their salaries have been stagnant or decreasing since the crisis, a development at a young age that has been shown to decrease earnings potential for workers even fifteen years later.[5]

At the same time, the cost for essentials is rising, making the effects of lower salaries all the more dramatic. Households are paying record fees for electricity, which has been consuming a greater share of Americans' after-tax income than at any time since 1996.[6] Food prices are also on the rise, hitting multi-decade highs, driven up by the impact of irregular weather patterns on supply, increasing demand from faster-growing nations, and speculation on commodities markets by investment banks ever since laws on the trading of commodities that could affect food prices were loosened in the early 2000s. Moreover, rents remain elevated, and in some cities they are even higher since the crisis, after many people lost homes they owned and were forced into the rental market. Nearly half of 25-to-34-year-olds living on their own in the United States spend more than a third of their income on rent. In big cities, the percentage is even higher.[7] And some landlords are tightening the criteria for rental applicants, requiring higher credit scores or higher deposits to secure an apartment, making it even more difficult for members of Generation Y to become or stay independent.

The upshot: the American dream, as we know it, is moving further and further out of reach for a generation that was pushed to achieve higher and higher levels of education to cash in on its promise but is now left asking, "What was it all for?" Generation Y is one of the most educated generations in history: 18 percent of 25-to-34-year-olds in the United States have a bachelor's degree, compared to 16 percent of 35-to-54-year-olds and 10.6 percent of people 55 and older.[8] But this a privilege it is paying for—and one that has not paid off as expected.

Heather Elizabeth was urged by her parents to get the best education money could buy. And why not? That's part of the American dream. She attended Middlebury College in Vermont, where the tuition is more than $53,000 per year, to study early childhood development and education.

To become a special education teacher, she needed a master's degree too. With her parents' encouragement, she again applied to the best schools in her field. She landed at Bank Street College in New York, a small and competitive school where annual tuition is more than $25,000, so Heather took out $17,000 in loans for graduate school.

What Heather didn't know is that her parents had already taken out about $20,000 in loans in order to pay for her top-notch undergraduate degree, a debt that is now in her name—all for a profession known for its relatively modest salary.

Now Heather is 25, living in Brooklyn, and married, and luckily she is working at a school doing the job she trained for. But her loan deferments are up, and it's time to start paying. In order to pay back as much as possible up front and not accrue higher interest payments, since the annual penalty payments on her loans rise each year, Heather has liquidated most of her assets. She has sapped all of her savings and a certificate of deposit, and sold all the stocks her relatives invested in for her when she was a child. Still, she owes about $20,000 on the principal of her loans, and much more with interest.

She and her husband, Ted, have very little financial cushion left should something unexpected happen. Plus, he's also a schoolteacher with another set of student loans. Living in New York on two modest teaching salaries is proving difficult. "We don't have much left over at the end of a month," said Heather.

She's looking ahead as Ted considers going back to school for a doctorate in education. "I'll need to find a new job, a challenge in this economy, clearly, pay for our health insurance, and cover whatever expenses we have."

Heather's story is not unusual. While college degrees are more important than ever to attaining a job in America, even a lower-skilled job that shouldn't require one, that education is also more expensive than ever. During the last thirty years, college tuition and fees have nearly tripled as universities take advantage of the rising demand, and scholarships and state funding can't keep up. Tuition is now the average American family's second-biggest investment, after their home. Total United States student loan debt is increasing at a rate of nearly $3,000 per second.[9] The average student loan debt today exceeds $25,000 and total outstanding loans topped $1 trillion for the first time.[10] The crisis has precipitated this trend, as more people are forced to go into debt.

Further illustrating the troubling effects, the Consumer Financial Protection Bureau solicited thousands of comments from consumers about their private student loans and published the comments in the summer of 2012. One commenter said: "I am 27 years old with a [bachelor of science] in meteorology. I currently work full-time in my field making $39,000 a year. I currently owe about $100,000 in student loans which most of it is private. I had no help from my family to pay for college so taking out a loan was my only option. . . . I paid about $10,000 in interest in 2011. That is 25.6 percent of my income. This is outrageous and something needs to be fixed. I am unable to consolidate for a lower rate because my debt to income ratio is too high. I did not qualify for Sallie Mae's lower interest program because I am able to currently maintain the payments. If nothing is done I will be done paying this in 2024 and would have paid over 100 percent of my original loan. I will be 39 years old. At that point I could start saving for a house. Lenders have way too much power and want people to default because they make more money that way."

But Millennials feel they have little choice but to go into debt for an education. The unemployment rate for college graduates is half that of those with only high school diplomas, and one-third of those with no diploma at all. Moreover, college graduates can expect to be paid almost twice as much as people with only high school diplomas—and those who attended graduate school can expect to earn two times more than that.[11] So for seemingly good reason, Millennials have been directed to go to college, and often graduate school, by any means necessary. They live in a system where a higher education is necessary for success.

The national drive for obtaining more and more education grew out of the shift in the United States from a manufacturing to a service sector economy. Just twenty years ago, America's largest corporations were led by manufacturing behemoths General Motors and Ford Motor. But the number of jobs they provided shrank over time, as new technologies reduced the need for some employees and manufacturing centers increasingly redistributed jobs to countries that had cheaper labor and materials than the United States, such as China and Vietnam. These were the middle-income jobs that used to finance the American dream for people who didn't graduate from college. But today the largest corporation is Walmart, and financial companies Berkshire Hathaway and Bank of America are also vying for top size. The service sector in fact represents almost 80 percent of the United States economy now, and is made up of jobs in government, telecommunications, the financial industry, retailers, and health care, among others. The result is that most post-baby-boom Americans need to go to college because most careers in the United States require a college diploma. America's shift has had a global impact too. The creation of new jobs in emerging-market countries, alongside broader globalization trends, has seen the growth of a middle class with more disposable income in those countries. That has encouraged companies to move not just manufacturing jobs to these developing markets but more and more of their business as well, as the middle class in America comes under financial strain. They are now shifting middle-income and even upper-income service sector jobs too, as corporations anticipate growing demand from these parts of the world. Unlike the United States, many emerging markets have been more resilient in the face of the Great Recession, accelerating this trend. In the past, companies that shifted service sector jobs overseas relocated American staff, but this is happening less and less. Western companies doing business in Asia are increasingly hiring locals to save money and take advantage of progress in education and experience in these emerging economies. An analysis of placements between 2005 and 2010 showed that three out of four senior executives hired in Asia by multinationals were Asian natives already living in the region.[12]

Overall, the workforce opportunities inside the United States are changing, and well-paid jobs with traditional employers are shrinking. According to the Bureau of Labor Statistics, seventeen million United States college graduates are working in jobs that require less education than a bachelor's degree, and unemployment among college graduates is the highest since 1970. Because of the crisis, the latest data in 2011 show that this is the first decade since 1941 in which more jobs were destroyed than created. The significance to Generation Y is that the United States just isn't producing the jobs and salaries to match the massive debts students are accruing. Amit Elhanan has fallen into this trap. He graduated from Rensselaer Polytechnic Institute, one of the top universities in the United States, and found a decent-paying job directly out of college at Infosys, a technology consultancy—a plum position for most young workers, especially given that he was $20,000 in debt for his education.

"If I would have stayed [at Infosys], I probably would have been a manager already, but I chose to go to law school," seeking what he thought could be even greater opportunities, said Amit.

As a member of Generation Y, he was guided throughout his life to chase his dreams. He wasn't satisfied by his job and wanted to go back to school and work in a career that mattered more to him, such as international policy. He chose law school over an immediate, stable income.

Amit attended Pace University Law School. It left him with an additional $170,000 in debt, which with his previous loans adds up to a $2,000 monthly payment. "That's crazy for someone right out of school," said Amit. "I am still living at home because with the cost of paying back my loans and rent, I am unable to move out right now. I am lucky enough to have parents who are okay with my staying here until I can move out."

People like Amit and Heather are indeed lucky. They have paying jobs and families to help support them. For many members of Generation Y, though, the glum employment environment means they can't afford to pay their loans at all and are wondering whether their education was worth it.

Besides the immediate stress and month-to-month financial

planning, high levels of debt so young in life sharply reduce one's credit score, which can have long-term consequences. Employers can refuse to hire workers with low credit scores, and they can also affect one's ability to rent or buy a home or a car. Credit card companies might refuse to grant these borrowers a credit line; if they do agree, the cost for that credit line (or any bank loans) will be much higher. Debtors also become ineligible for more student loans, just in case they were thinking another type of degree or education could provide a better income to help get them out of their debt hole. Debts owed to the government could result in their salary and any tax refunds being seized. Moreover, government-funded student loans can't just be cleared through bankruptcy like a home loan, and rarely do private creditors allow student loans to be discharged because creditors say those taking out student loans should end up earning more later on as a direct result of their education. The borrower—be it the student or parents—must deal with the debt for life. Loans to parents for the college education of their children have jumped 75 percent over the past five years. In many cases, the parents are close to retirement and facing their own loan repayments, but with depleted savings after the crisis they are forced to take out more loans to support their children.[13]

"Income tax debt can be discharged. Small-business loans can be discharged. I can help them get rid of their other debts. For those who come into my office, and the only problem is, 'I got a $30,000 student loan, what can you do for me?' I pretty much say, 'Nothing,'" said William E. Brewer Jr., president of the National Association of Consumer Bankruptcy Attorneys. He says that Congress should allow college debts to be forgiven and reintroduce a statute of limitations on the length of time a creditor has to sue a borrower after defaulting, as it was in the 1970s. In the 1990s, new laws eliminated any statute of limitations on student loans, so a graduate could be in default for fifteen years and suddenly get sued by a loan company. In contrast, even lawsuits for medical malpractice have a statute of limitations, usually around three years.

"You either pay them or get sued," said William. "And some of the student loan agencies are the ugliest, and the reason is all you can do is run and hide. The loan can't be discharged."

The student loan landscape is an increasing risk to the United States economy itself. It is already expanding the opportunity gap between the rich and middle class: the risk of being unable to pay back loans will deter young people from taking them out, and soon only those born into wealthy families will have access to higher education. As the cost of college becomes increasingly misaligned with its value, it is on track to be the next asset bubble to burst after the housing market—and this time the government is directly on the hook. The percentage of student borrowers defaulting on their federal loans two years after graduating has risen to multiyear highs, reaching 10 percent, as the size of the loans also increases. But longer-term analysis by the *Chronicle of Higher Education* paints a more dramatic picture: the default rate over the life of a college loan is actually double that, closer to 20 percent. That's a higher default rate than with any other type of loan available in the United States, and one of the only types of loan markets that has increased in size since the financial crisis spurred consumers to save more and borrow less.[14] Education is not typically one of those things that Americans try to scrimp on. The potential crisis plays out like this: One out of every five people taking out an education loan—and most college students must take out loans, and now most people need to go to college—won't be able to meet the repayment schedule. As the economy slowly improves and the central bank raises the interest rate for borrowing back above the record lows of the post-crisis period, the rate of default on these loans could snowball. Fears are growing that billions of dollars just won't be repaid, leaving a huge hole in the United States economy. The risk doesn't end there. There is a whole securities market that has developed around student loans, just like the housing market, although it is smaller. It's easy to see how the scenario would unfold. Ironically, Fitch Ratings, a credit rating agency that scores the safety of such investments, assured clients in 2012 that while asset-backed securities tied to private sector loans could be risky, securities tied to federal loans are still safe because they are backed by the Family Federal Education Program. Translation: taxpayers would have to bail out investors in a federal program, so go ahead, investors, and expand that market.

Why has the cost of the American dream of a college degree gotten so high for Generation Y anyway? From 1990 to 2010, tuition and fees at public four-year universities more than doubled and the prices of two-year colleges climbed by 71 percent, while median household income rose just 2 percent.[15] This increase is primarily the result of lower endowments and subsidies from the government due to budget cuts, which increase the burden on schools to raise money themselves. Real funding per public full-time student dropped by 26 percent between 1990 and 2010, according to think tank Demos. As schools receive less money from the state, they must charge students more for the education. Colleges are also spending more to attract top administrators and professors. But many of those professors prefer to focus on their own personal research rather than teach students, which means the schools need to pay for more staff to meet classroom needs. Tuition is also a means for competition between universities. Andrew Manshel, who once served as the vice president of finance and administration at Barnard College, explained the price-setting process: "I was surprised to learn from my colleagues that tuition and fees were not set by analyzing budget projections. Instead they were set by looking at a chart of the prior year's tuition charges at comparable schools and then trying to predict their increases for the next year. The goal was to maintain the college's position in the pecking order of total charges."[16] Rising tuitions, whatever the reason, have not deterred college applicants. To be sure, America has a high concentration of the best universities in the world, institutions that overall arm the country's young with unparalleled training in critical thinking. But the costs just don't make sense. According to the Delta Cost Project, which analyzes college costs versus productivity, the cost to a public college or university for providing instruction for the average bachelor's degree is between $25,000 and $40,000, covered by a mix of public subsidies and student tuition. By contrast, the average cost for a student to obtain a degree from a public institution is between $35,000 and $70,000.[17]

For all of these reasons, it is not, as some pundits have argued, that an entire generation doesn't want to or know how to grow up. It is simply becoming too difficult—prohibitively expensive—to achieve key rites of passage. The transition to adulthood is becoming a greater challenge, and as a result Generation Y's independence has been a major casualty of the crisis.

Since the crisis, a quarter of young adults reported delaying marriage and about one-third have delayed starting a family. Almost half of young adults have also delayed purchasing a home, and nearly one-third of young people have delayed moving out of their family home.[18] The economic downturn has fueled the largest increase in modern history in the number of Americans living in multigenerational households, as Millennials put off moving out of their parents' homes or move back into them after high school or college.[19] It is a stress on the entire family, since the net worth of baby boomer parents has also declined since the crisis, with many losing their jobs on the cusp of retirement and finding it hard to secure a spot in the workplace again. American families' median net worth fell from $126,400 in 2007 to $77,300 in 2010, representing a 40 percent drop.[20]

Nicholas and Katie DeVito are a prime example. They were forced to move in with his parents in Hamilton, New Jersey, in 2009, when they were laid off from their jobs in human resources and nonprofit management within just months of each other. More than two years later, both are still without work. Katie is attempting to start her own business as a social media expert, helping other unemployed people find opportunities. Nicholas is still searching, and all the while responsible for paying off student loans from his undergraduate and master's degrees.

"We'd love to be able to move out and get a house and

have kids. I mean, I'm 33 years old. But we don't want to get kids until we get the house," said Katie. "Plus, we don't have the money. We don't have health insurance."

Nicholas and Katie illustrate another trend that has been little discussed: the financial crisis has led to a significant drop in birth rates, as "growing up," in the traditional sense, becomes harder to do for would-be parents. Beyond the personal effect on members of Generation Y, who were hoping to build a family but are instead waiting with anxiety until the moment that the math makes better sense, the big picture result of a declining birth rate means that there will be fewer people to grow the economy and absorb the costs of government spending in an aging United States population.

In 2007, before the financial crisis began taking its toll, the United States saw a record high number of births— more than 4 million. Just two years later, that number has dropped to the lowest in more than half a decade. It's not a coincidence. Pew Research discovered that the states experiencing the largest economic declines in 2007 and 2008 were most likely to experience relatively large fertility declines from 2008 to 2009. After all, the cost of having a child is rising, despite the global downturn: in addition to the rising cost of food and household necessities, center-based child care fees for two children now exceed annual median rent payments.[21]

"My grandma, who is 95 years old and lived through the Great Depression, said to me: 'I can't imagine what you guys are going through and how you are this young and dealing with this sort of stuff so early on in your life . . . You're married and you want to have a house and kids,'" said Katie.

Her grandmother worked, got married, had children, stayed home with them, and then went back to work again. She was never without a job until she retired. She worked at the same company for years and never experienced lay-offs. The contrast between her life and Katie's is stark.

"'How do you start life like that?' my grandma asked me," said Katie. Katie herself is unsure.

Some young couples take a makeshift route.

Nearly a year into their marriage, Adam and Ashley Deutsch, both 27, moved into a veritable fraternity house— eight bedrooms and seven other roommates, all medical school students. It wasn't private or romantic, or how they imagined starting a life together. But they had few options. Adam had just graduated from law school at Seton Hall in May 2010 and Ashley was still studying at the University of Medicine and Dentistry of New Jersey in Newark. Because of the crisis, Adam had no clear employment prospects.

"Everyone hears 'doctor' and 'lawyer' and thinks we are set for life, but the reality is that as a couple who really wants to have kids and build a family, we carry a boatload of student debt that stands to prevent us from achieving many of our goals," said Adam. "Both of us will tell anyone thinking of entering our professions that if they are attracted by income, there are more efficient ways to get there."

"All of our adult relatives thought we were insane: a newlywed couple moving in with a group of people who I barely knew," said Adam. But he and his wife saw it as being practical. Instead of paying $1,500 in rent for their South Orange, New Jersey, apartment, they were able to cut the monthly cost to $750 in a crowded house in the neighboring town of Orange. However, they were living like college students, not independent adults.

Eventually Adam found work in one of the many law firms that have popped up to counter the effects of the crisis: he defends those in foreclosure lawsuits or on the verge of default, and sues brokers and lenders for predatory lending. After feeling the direct effects of the crisis, he began to see how it was hurting other people's lives too, and he was able to help them. Asked if the experience has scared him off from buying a home, Adam responded emphatically: "Yes, it definitely makes me more cautions." This fear, not just of buying a home but of taking out any loans or taking on any other financial risk, is a persistent effect of the crisis on many in Generation Y—and could have long-term economic consequences on the growth of the United States economy. Not that the opportunity to buy a home is so easily available.

For those young people who want to buy a home now, the financial crisis has made it increasingly difficult to secure financing, despite historically low interest rates on home loans. Besides unstable job prospects, and therefore unsteady or low wages, bank standards for obtaining that loan are much higher than before the crisis. Banks now ask for proof of income and sometimes want to see evidence of high levels of income growth, with some lenders even asking for third parties to verify that documents aren't fake. Though mortgage standards in the past were too lenient and likely contributed to the creation of the housing bubble, the pendulum has now swung far in the opposite direction. And even though salaries have held steady or decreased, housing prices are steadily recovering in most key American cities.[22]

The inability to buy a home not only excludes this generation of young adults from one of our country's major rites of passage but burdens them with additional financial difficulties. The United States tax system is built on the premise of an indebted population of homeowners. For instance, homeowners can deduct the cost of mortgage payments from their taxes, and parents are awarded deductions for their children, both of which are meant to secure the American dream of home ownership and two and a half kids. The tax system doesn't take into account the changing realities in America that are forcing that dream to change—a shift that Federal Reserve chairman Ben Bernanke confirmed in a 2012 report to the House of Representatives' Committee on Financial Services, which addressed lenders' declining risk profiles and the difficulty in accessing mortgage credit: "Indeed, if the currently prevailing standards had been in place during the past few decades, a larger portion of the nation's housing stock probably would have been designed and built for rental, rather than owner occupancy."

Ultimately, all of the problems accelerated by the financial crisis—unemployment and lower wages, delayed milestones, student loan debt and high college tuitions—are rooted in a single culprit. For decades, the United States has been singularly focused on the baby boomers, spending more money, energy, and time to support the nation's aging population than its young. Even before the crisis broke out, Mr. Bernanke warned about this in a speech that asked, "Will we treat future generations fairly?" He concluded, "A failure on our part to prepare for demographic change will have substantial adverse effects on the economic welfare of our children and grandchildren and on the long-run productive potential of the U.S. economy."[23]

If the federal budget is a barometer for national priorities, then it's all the evidence that is necessary. In the typical federal budget, about 20 percent is allocated to social security for the aging population and 13 percent is allocated to Medicare, the government-run health insurance program for those 65 and older. And at the current rate, spending on Medicare and social security will increase from about 10 percent of gross domestic product (GDP) to 16 percent over the next twenty-five years. In comparison, just 2 percent of the budget is set aside for scientific research and 3 percent for education, training, and employment programs. Deep budget cuts at the federal and state levels in the aftermath of the financial crisis have made these already anemic programs even less effective, putting Generation Y's prospects at further risk. There simply will not be enough money in the United States' coffers to continue funding these programs when Generation Y is ready to retire from working. Making the situation even more dire, more than one-third of the federal budget is financed by borrowing. This is a bill Generation Y will have to pay in the future. Until then, about 6 percent of the budget today is used to pay the interest on that debt—that's double the budget for education.

Uthman Baksh, 22, is a full-time college student in New York with a part-time job that barely pays for his living expenses. Since enrolling at Brooklyn College nearly four years ago to study psychology, he has seen his government-funded financial aid cut every year. Tuition costs, meanwhile, are on the rise. This has made him question whether he can afford to go on to graduate school—which students are told can help them secure a better job down the line—and if he will earn enough afterward to pay for all these accruing debts. "I do plan on going to graduate school but

I want to do it in order to get a job and a career," he said, as opposed to more debt with no reward at the end. Uthman is suffering under the axe of education budget cuts, and his story illustrates how America has failed to prioritize its future generations—and how the situation has become worse since the crisis.

Priorities at the state level reflect the same philosophy. Additional state budget cuts to higher education are foreseen as the United States continues to rein in spending, which may result in more tuition hikes despite lower personal incomes. And at the primary and secondary school levels, the pressures continue. Consider Anne Delagdo, 30, a teacher in Madison, Wisconsin, caught in a war between the state's government and her union. Because of a strained budget, the state is asking teachers to make unprecedented sacrifices in their bargaining rights, benefits, and salaries. The cuts touch how much time teachers have to prepare for classes and resources too. Anne has been participating in protests against the reforms with colleagues from across the state, which hasn't seen a teacher union strike since the 1970s.

"We're already getting by with very little. Madison is on the lower side of school funding," she said. Still, Anne is realistic about the outlook, given the post-crisis economic climate: "There are a lot of things we can't avoid."

The cuts don't have to come down this way, though. These policy arrangements are the product of a different society, a different economy, which has since evolved. Old promises seem irrelevant today, and we need to refocus on the future.

"We basically have middle-age consumption systems," said Eugene Steuerle, Richard B. Fisher Chair at the Urban Institute, referring to payouts to the aging population and government subsidies for families who can afford to own homes or have children. "There is no reason we couldn't put more subsidies into the young and jobs, except we've promised it elsewhere—and that's the political problem." Our politicians are making promises aimed at capturing the votes of the large and influential baby boomer demographic that is transitioning into retirement. That is a big part of the reason so much of the federal budget goes to social security and Medicare. But the growing costs are terrifying. There are now forty million people in the United States who are 65 or older, and this number is seen more than doubling by 2050 as baby boomers age. Most of this increase will take place over the next twenty years, at the same time as the nation tries to recover from the financial crisis. This will place a strain on state budgets and public services, especially amid higher obesity and disability rates, and turn social security, Medicare, and Medicaid into unsustainable programs that Generation Y will be unable to utilize.[24]

But the political promises extend elsewhere as well, undercutting proper policy planning for the country's future. The country's politicians are indebted not only to the boomers but also to other major voting blocs, donors to political campaigns and political action committees (PACs), and lobbyists. For instance, during the crisis, the government focused on bailing out failing sectors of the economy such as the automobile industry at least in part because of its large and influential lobby. In one of the clearest examples, the energy industry and other business groups spent billions of dollars to lobby lawmakers for the construction of the Keystone XL oil pipeline, which became the center of a national debate after legislators tied its construction first to a tax cut law and then to a desperately needed jobs bill. Lobbies play a huge role in directing economic policy in America, and there isn't one strong enough battling for the economic interests of Generation Y. Politicians regularly outright ask lobby groups for donations and spend a very large portion of their time attending fund-raisers and meeting lobbyists in the hopes of getting more money for their next election campaign. John McCain, who served as senator for the state of Arizona and was a Republican presidential nominee in 2008, told the radio program *This American Life*: "It's the system and the water in which we swim."[25] Money comes from individual and corporate donors too. And ever since the Supreme Court in 2010 opened the way to allow limitless amounts of money to be donated toward politicians and their causes via "super PACs," the influence of small groups on issues that affect the entire population has grown.

What politicians seem to be forgetting is that investing in Generation Y's future—with initiatives such as education programs, work subsidies, paid apprenticeships, and scientific research funding—benefits society as a whole. For example, the more educated a person is, the less likely that person is to need unemployment benefits or welfare assistance. In addition, those with college degrees pay more taxes when they enter the job market. According to the OECD, a man with a college diploma will pay an average of $91,000 in income taxes and social contributions over his working life. That's not a bad return on investment, and it's why the government should agree to subsidize more college educations, encourage companies to hire young workers by subsidizing the cost of employing recent graduates, and protect Generation Yers from unpaid or low-paid positions.

The underinvestment in Generation Y, particularly

during the Great Recession and its fallout, is a bitter pill for many Millennials to swallow after they carried Barack Obama to victory in the 2008 presidential election. President Obama received the highest share of the youth vote obtained by any candidate on record: 68 percent. Yet to many young adults, he seems unconcerned with Generation Y's inheritance, namely, a giant debt load and the shadow of a thriving economy, or its politicization.

Charles Henry, 26, was one of many Millennials fired up by Obama's "hope and change" rhetoric during the election. Today, that flame of admiration and hope is extinguished, mostly because of Obama's response to the financial crisis.

"He did definitely talk a good line during the campaign," but when the crisis hit, the president should have launched a debt relief program for young people, said Charles. He also criticized the president's proposal to allow companies to hire young workers for free, reinforcing their low value in the workplace, while the government offered them only a modest stipend. Charles says the president failed him and others like him. He and other supporters were willing to ignore the fact that Obama raised more money from Wall Street than other candidates, and he believed the president would stimulate the economy and take care of its citizens. Instead, Obama bailed out banks but refused to help ordinary people, said Charles, who works in advertising and lives in New York. His disappointment drove him to get involved in Occupy Wall Street, where Charles contributes to alternative proposals for the United States banking system and economic policies along with a small group of educated and committed volunteers.

Cheyenna Weber, a 29-year-old activist originally

from West Virginia, was also inspired by President Obama's experience as a community organizer and his campaign promises to end the war in Iraq, hold banks and corporations accountable, and provide what she calls "economic justice" for American citizens. She was so inspired, in fact, that Cheyenna led the front desk of his campaign in New York, directing office visitors where to go and answering telephones.

"It became my full-time job in the last few weeks before the election. I won't make that mistake again," said Cheyenna. "My running joke about the election is that as consumers, there are laws about bait and switch, but with politicians you don't have that."

In the end, Generation Y is left questioning America's future and our role in it. Our chance at a higher education seems to move further away, even as that education becomes increasingly important to success, and the burden of student debt is overwhelming. The number of jobs available to Gen Yers is shrinking. We were taught to chase our dreams but are facing a troubling reality instead. And as we come of age, it is increasingly clear that we are on the bottom of a long list of priorities. But by not prioritizing young people, America's leaders risk creating a lost generation—a risk that could become a pandemic across the richest countries in the world.

2

Europe in Crisis

I am mindful of the sacrifices some of these reforms imply for the Portuguese population in the short term. But as Fernando Pessoa has written into the logbook of the Portuguese nation of seafarers: "There are ships sailing to many ports, but not a single one goes where life is not painful."

—European economics commissioner Olli Rehn, March 15, 2012, reviewing Portugal's progress in implementing budget cuts to meet the demands of its bailout program

Judging by the evidence that we have, austerity programs in Europe and elsewhere appear likely to yield disappointing results.

—Economist Robert Shiller, "Does Austerity Promote Economic Growth?" January 18, 2012

The economic turmoil that spread from the United States dramatically affected Generation Y across Europe as well. But leaders there made the problem worse for Millennials when they attempted to tackle the biggest threat to their economies since World War II with a coordinated program of austerity measures—some combination of reduced spending and higher taxes to lower deficits. As a result, one out of every five young people is out of work. The outlook for jobs and economic success is even worse than in the United States.

Ludovica Rogers knows the consequences of the austerity policies all too well. For the past three years, she has traveled around the European Union trying to find its last remaining job opportunities. She's come up empty.

She has one bachelor's degree in math and physics from University College London, another in architecture from Politecnico di Milano in Italy, and a master's degree in architecture and urbanism from Technische Universiteit Delft in the Netherlands. Immediately after graduating in 2007—when the global economy was still strong—she found an internship designing residential villas in the Netherlands. Hoping to take the next step in her career, she moved to another small architecture firm in Berlin, working as a freelancer to collaborate with engineers and architects in the United Arab Emirates on a plan for a sustainable development in Dubai. When the project wrapped up, Ludovica decided to leave Berlin because there was little room for professional growth at that firm. The world over, young people have little choice today but to hop from one company to another to climb up the ladder, unlike the past, when people received promotions and raises for service, loyalty, and experience. Ludovica thought work outside of Europe might enhance her resume for potential employers and she tried to find a position in Chile for a few months. But all the work was unpaid, so she returned to Europe and stayed in her parents' home in Milan.

It was now January 2008, and she started applying everywhere she could. She thought it was tough to get ahead before, but while she was gone, the job market collapsed, along with the housing market as bank financing tightened. Ludovica sent applications to at least 150 firms in two months and received zero responses. "Everyone I knew basically had lost their job in architecture," she said. "Not only was there no work, but there were so many unemployed people applying for jobs." She stayed in Italy for two years and couldn't find a single job. She started her own firm just so she could enter architecture design contests, not actually expecting to get paying work. The situation across Europe was so desperate, though, that suddenly Ludovica started receiving job applications from other people to work at her "firm," which made no income.

Then in 2010 and 2011, austerity measures started sweeping across much of Europe. Italy came under the knife of budget cuts, which made businesses even more nervous to hire, and sent youth unemployment levels up. Thinking a move to the Netherlands might help reboot her career, Ludovica packed her bags again. She rented an apartment with her savings and applied for another one hundred jobs. She found one internship that paid €600 per month. However, it was a fixed contract for just three months. "It was so frustrating to be working as an intern. I was 30 years old," said Ludovica.

She packed once more and relocated to London, where she could stay for free in an apartment her parents owned and rented out to students. Again, she sent out a mass mailing of resumes to London architecture firms. By now she had been out of work for three years, living off money her grandfather left after passing away. However, she's moved around so much—which European officials encourage and say is the key advantage of the European Union—that she hasn't been able to apply for social benefits in any country, because you cannot carry accrued benefits across borders even if it is inside the economic bloc. "The answers here in London are all the same. They receive hundreds of applications every single day," said Ludovica. "You realize it's not your fault. I realize I'm extremely lucky I have family behind me."

The experience has been a real eye-opener for Ludovica. She's given up searching for work for a while and has refocused on volunteering for the Occupy movement in London, helping to organize events and the group's communications. She earns extra money now and then by analyzing the energy efficiency of apartments in Milan.

"I'm in a bit of a crisis phase at the moment," said Ludovica.

Youth across Europe are in crisis.

The youth unemployment rate has increased by 50 percent since 2008, rising every year, and as time goes by it will become harder to reverse the trend. The immediate blow of the financial crisis contributed significantly, but in the midst of turmoil leaders have had other matters on their mind. During the crisis, the cost for governments to borrow money on financial markets started to rise amid fears of default, as national debts ballooned. Investors feared they wouldn't be repaid. A system based on trust was falling apart. Part of their concern was that the euro zone's central bank, an institution shared between seventeen member states, wouldn't take extreme enough measures to support just a few of those states in need of assistance, and the stronger economies wouldn't condone bailing out the failing countries. By comparison, the United States Treasury worked side by side with the Federal Reserve during the crisis to take unconventional measures, including injecting more money into the economy. Investors were uncertain euro zone countries would work the same way with the European Central Bank, which has a reputation for being much more conservative with its powers. Moreover, all the member states must make decisions concerning the region's economy together, and investors doubted they would be able to make measurable unanimous decisions. The higher the perceived risk of loaning money to certain countries, the higher the borrowing rates for those countries grew. And the fear spread. From one country to another, investors turned cautious. The borrowing rates escalated to unsustainable levels. Credit rating agencies, long silent on the risks of too-high government debt in the developed world, started to send warnings to market participants. Governments had to take aggressive and immediate action to prevent chaos—either a disorderly default to investors, failing to meet financial obligations to public sector workers and the running of government, or both.

In order to reduce their debts and deficits, and to show investors that they could reform their economies, nearly every European Union government committed to an austerity scheme. They thought this policy could spur growth and confidence again. In some countries, like Greece, Spain, and Ireland, the measures have been dramatic. However, government budget cuts during times of crisis, when money among consumers and businesses is already tight and confidence is already low, have a high price because the government is further reducing resources that those businesses and consumers should be using to make the economy run and grow. Eventually, without this input in the form of buying or hiring, the economy stops running normally and starts panting. By implementing these reforms before an economy fully recovers from a crisis, leaders can totally constrict economic growth. And that's exactly what happened in Europe. Economic growth became so depressed that leaders actually inadvertently caused a second recession in several countries just a few years after the first, with the costs of high unemployment and reduced income disproportionately falling on the shoulders of young people, which European Central Bank president Mario Draghi even acknowledged in comments to the European Parliament in Brussels in January 2012.

Research from the International Monetary Fund in 2011 pointed to Europe's erroneous thinking. In the IMF's quarterly magazine, *Finance & Development*, IMF economists Daniel Leigh and Prakash Loungani, with Johns Hopkins University economics professor Laurence Ball, warned about the adverse impact on growth and jobs. They examined 173 austerity episodes over the past thirty years in seventeen advanced economies, including Australia, Austria, Belgium, Canada, Denmark, Finland, France, Germany, Ireland, Italy, Japan, the Netherlands, Portugal, Spain, Sweden, the United Kingdom, and the United States. Their evidence showed that austerity reduced incomes and raised unemployment in the short term, contrasting with earlier suggestions that cutting the budget deficit can spur growth in the short term. Moreover, the effects become all the more pronounced when many countries do this at the same time, as in the case of Europe. That means that austerity measures taken today are likely to be even more contractionary on an economy than the economists' historical examples are able to show. On top of that, the negative effects continue into the future. Fiscal contractions undercut job hopes for the long-term unemployed, when someone is out of work for more than six months, according to the study.[1] The problem is that leaders confused reform and austerity, says Amartya Sen, winner of the 1998 Nobel Memorial Prize in Economic Sciences: "Nothing in Europe is as important today as a clear-headed recognition of what has gone so badly wrong in implementing the grand vision of a united Europe."[2]

European governments did not take advantage of the good times to make the necessary reforms to balance their federal budgets—nor did the United States. From the mid-1980s up until 2007, economic growth, industrial production, inflation, and employment were mostly stable. The period was so secure that it became known as the Great Moderation or the Great Stability. And great economists, such as Nobel Prize winner Robert Lucas, hailed macroeconomics as a success in preventing depressions and suggested that studies should move on to other challenges.[3] United States Federal Reserve chairman Ben Bernanke gave a famous speech during this period, similarly arguing that the reduced economic volatility could be partly credited to better monetary policy by central bankers. This made him optimistic for the future, thinking that perhaps macroeconomists had learned from past economic events how to prevent crises.[4] But an analysis by economists at the Federal Reserve today shows how shortsighted such views were: "In sum, our calculations suggest that the Great Recession was indeed entirely off the radar of a standard macroeconomic model estimated with data drawn exclusively from the Great Moderation. By contrast, the extreme events of 2008–09 are seen as far from impossible—if unlikely—by the same model when the shocks hitting the economy are gauged using data from a longer period (third-quarter 1954 to fourth-quarter 2007). These results provide a simple quantitative illustration of the extent to which the Great Moderation, and more specifically the assumption that the tranquil environment characterizing it was permanent, might have led economists to greatly underestimate the possibility of a Great Recession." Many now suggest that confidence during the Great Moderation also led governments to accommodate financial markets by encouraging investors and banks to take more risks, paving the way for the crisis.

They were the glory days of low interest rates and high growth, but then policy makers screwed up. Governments in Europe and the United States should have acted back then to balance their budgets, change tax systems, and alter spending obligations in order to strengthen their economies and protect them from crisis. But nobody wanted to rock the boat. Jean Claude Juncker, prime minister of Luxembourg and a key player in the European debt crisis drama, famously summed it up: "We all know what to do, we just don't know how to get re-elected after we've done it." It's not a politician's job to be an economist or even think about the future. A politician's job is to win votes in order to keep his or her post.

Now, however, there is an imperative to tighten budgets fast. Could governments have at least taken a less aggressive route in the aftermath of the crisis? Top think tanks, including the OECD, say Europe should have constructed a better mix of policies in the aftermath of the crisis—a recovery road map that prioritized growth and job creation as much as balancing the governments' checkbooks—to avoid the fallout that has been paralyzing for an entire generation of would-be entrepreneurs, scientists, and doers. Voters seem to think so too. In 2012 elections, the electorate lashed out against the austerity-supporting parties in

Greece, France, and Italy, in the clearest sign since their budget-cutting campaign began that patience for such policies are fading fast, as the promise of economic recovery seems to move further and further into the future. Unfortunately, while the changing tide may finally push leaders to adjust their course, the effects of their measures thus far will be lasting.

Staggering Unemployment Ravages Spain

In Spain, every other person under 25 years old is out of work. Every third person between the ages of 25 and 35 is out of work. As their time out of school and work increases, their value to the workplace and their salaries for years to come decrease. And the country's debt-to-GDP ratio threatens to veer still higher, as economic growth remains low after painful budget cuts and reforms that have affected the entire population, and especially Generation Y's potential for a fair livelihood. That's left many young people in Spain asking the government, "Was it all worth it?"

"When we are trying to explain our situation, we can explain the facts. But it's kind of difficult to explain what we feel," said Èric Lluent, a young journalist who launched the blog *Els Nous Pobres*, or *New Poor People*, with his childhood friend Santiago Pérez. On the website, unemployed people can post their personal stories of struggle. "It's shocking and it's frustrating. It means that every morning you wake up and you don't have anything to do. You can go to run. You can meet some friends. But you don't have a job. You don't have some goal in your life. It's difficult to have a goal in your life if you don't have money. You feel trapped. There are small things, like I can't buy my nephew a present. But there are many, many of these small things. I'm not depressed, but I feel depressed sometimes."

At the age of 16, Èric was already getting regular jobs as a journalist, creating segments for radio stations and writing articles for newspapers. It was his dream, and because university classes hampered his work, he quit two years into his degree.

"My mom has no job. My father works in a low-class job, maybe getting a little bit more than €1,000 per month. My family is not so rich. I felt that it would be fair that I should start to work and get my own money—and I found jobs so quickly," said Èric.

"I remember I was 19 years old and I was getting €600. It was not so much, but now it is impossible to get that to make a radio program. I was planning to work in many places and do many things and write in many newspapers. You never expect that you will lose all this," he said.

In 2008, Spain's housing sector collapsed. It employed a disproportionate size of the workforce and had its tentacles across the entire economy. Builders, real estate agents, materials suppliers—they all lost out on work. These companies stopped advertising in media, including the newspapers and radio stations Èric wrote for; those media outlets began to fail as well. Construction at building sites stalled, hurting local businesses. People could no longer pay back the loans on overpriced apartments and houses. Then the banks and corporations exposed to the once-booming sector also came under pressure, many going into bankruptcy. It was a giant domino game that toppled.

Like others, Èric was in shock and out of work. The radio stations stopped calling. The newspapers didn't have enough money to contract him for articles. He decided to leave Spain and move to Helsinki, Finland, to try to start a new life. But he couldn't find work there either. He moved on to Iceland and got an internship in Reykjavik. It was a summer contract that ended with no prospects for renewal. So Èric returned home to Barcelona. He tried to find work in a bar or restaurant, but the positions were incredibly competitive.

Now he's 25 years old and remains out of regular work. Èric occasionally gets an article published but is usually just paid about €40 for the work. That's barely enough for food. He lives with his parents. He tried to go back to university, but he can't secure financial support from the government for books and travel expenses. Like others, Èric feels lost in life.

The outlook for Generation Y grew even darker in Spain when the government imposed severe budget cuts to try to cover national debts following the housing collapse and boost financial market confidence, in part to meet European Union targets. As a member of the European Union, Spain is obligated to meet certain economic targets, for the health of neighboring countries closely connected to its economy, if not for its own economic stability.

For the general population, the budget reforms have meant less hiring and more firing, a 5 percent to 15 percent cut in salaries, rescinded tax breaks, laws that make it easier for private employers to pay workers less and lay them off, a much smaller government workforce, and a reduction in public funding to education, research, housing, unemployment, and maternity programs.

Advertised as a means to strengthen the economy, these reforms did little to build a better foundation for Generation Y. In addition to slashing jobs, they failed to address problems that have long haunted Spain's youngest workers. They failed to increase resources to train the unemployed or change the country's dual labor market, where youth are markedly underprotected compared to older workers and are often stuck in unstable and temporary contracts. At the beginning of the crisis, 35 percent of all workers were on such temporary contracts—most of them young people. Economists say their tenuous positions contributed to Spain's job crisis because workers are not encouraged to seek education or training if they know the payoff will just be transient work. It also keeps a constant level of unemployment built into the labor market.

Veronica Leandrez learned about the devastation in Spain the hard way. She graduated from Tulane University in New Orleans in 2001 with a degree in fine arts. Until the United States market crash seven years later, she mostly earned a steady salary selling paintings and drawings, as well as creating theater backdrops. In 2008, her income took a severe hit. Commissions stopped coming. After months of searching for theater jobs or any other art-related work—with the unemployment rate hovering near 10 percent—Veronica decided to move to her parents' old house in Castilla–La Mancha, Spain, where she was born 33 years earlier. Veronica did not anticipate what awaited her.

"Mostly everybody that I've met is unemployed," she said.

Veronica, who didn't have any more luck in Spain than in New Orleans finding work or art buyers, joined the *Indignados*, the "indignant ones," a group of protesters angry with the state of the Spanish economy.

Together with fifty other men and women, mostly in

their twenties and thirties, Veronica participated in a one-thousand-mile march from Madrid to Brussels, the European Union's political capital, to call attention to the plight of the unemployed and those targeted by government budget cuts. It did not convince leaders to soften the reforms.

Now, said Veronica, "I am here for the Spanish revolution." Like others protesting throughout Europe—such as in Athens and Rome—Veronica feels marginalized by the unfairness of the situation. A huge part of the population that had little, if any, part in creating the financial crisis is now expected to pay a huge price for the mess left by their elders, with consequences that may last a lifetime.

Fidel Romero helped launch the *Indignado* protest movement in Seville in southwest Spain. In the beginning there were just ten to twenty members. A few months later, everything exploded. By October of 2011, a march in Seville attracted some forty thousand participants, say local sources.

"Most people want to have at least the minimum rights. Now there is a problem with jobs. There is a problem with houses; the banks are taking the houses. When humans don't have a home or a job or something to eat, then the problems come," said Fidel. "I know a lot of people in our movement who have to go every day to a social institution to eat."

Fidel is 32 years old, is fluent in English and learning Chinese and French, and holds a degree in law from the Universidad Pablo de Olavide in Seville. He didn't particularly like law but thought the degree would offer him good job opportunities and security. After the crisis struck, he lost his job in a real estate company's legal department. Despite his skill set, he hasn't been able to find any work since—not in his field, or even as a waiter, a telephone operator at a call center, or a taxi driver. He wants to work for a nongovernmental organization, but none of the local do-good groups have any money to hire people because their funding from the state was cut off. Fidel lives with his mother and she supports him financially, which is a burden since her own salary has been reduced by 10 percent.

Spain's troubles have turned the view of the *mileuristas* epidemic on its head. Before, economists and journalists highlighted this set of highly educated young people who don't earn more than €1,000 per month as a growing problem for the country and its future leaders. Now, though, many are thankful to be earning even that much. For instance, since losing his teaching job and research grant in Spanish history at the University of Santiago de Compostela, Álvaro Rodriguez, now 34, doesn't know what he'll do next. He can't find any work and has moved back in with his parents. He already tried starting his own business while he worked at the university. He created an online publishing company for academic research before the crisis. But it was impossible to get a loan from local banks for anything other than construction projects, without putting up his family's home as collateral. Now it's nearly impossible to get a loan, period. Banks are hoarding cash because they have to build up their capital buffers to meet the demands of new laws aimed at protecting the financial system against the threat of another crisis. They are also fearful that the economic instability introduced by budget cuts could worsen the country's outlook. It's a self-fulfilling cycle that is cutting off opportunities for Álvaro and his peers.

"What we feel is all these economic policies are against the people. . . . We are living some kind of precarious existence, and we can't make our own home or have a traditional career like our parents," said Alvaro. "The only field that has increased the budget here is the police." He would know. His father is the town's police chief. Indeed, it might be a worthwhile budget decision. Studies show that youth unemployment increases the risk of crime and substance use, and is consistently associated with criminal damage and robbery rates.[5]

The anxiety in Spain has trickled down to the very young too. Lauren Sieben is an American who has been teaching students in a Seville high school.

"A lot of them, even at about 13 years old, are already jaded. They're watching their parents and family members lose jobs and they're wondering what exactly they're in school for, especially if they're not going to find work with or without a degree later on," she said.

A Generation in Greece Caught in a Tragedy

From violent protests on the streets of Athens—where democracy began—to the new poor quietly trying to get by, perhaps no country has been as devastated by the crisis and attendant austerity measures as Greece, where the unemployment rate for youth is more than 50 percent.

So far, the government has cut public sector wages by more than 30 percent and instituted wage freezes. Many private companies have followed suit. The government also reduced the minimum wage by more than 20 percent, and by more than 30 percent for those under the age of 25. Pensions have been slashed and taxes have been hiked. Tens of thousands of civil servant jobs have been suspended, and all temporary contracts, which were mostly held by young people, were eliminated. Costs have increased for utilities and food. This all threatens the chance of economic mobility and success for Greece's young workforce, and results in fewer opportunities for Generation Y. Moreover, this hopelessness has a fed a growing neo-Nazi movement, known as the Golden Dawn, and increased crime on the streets, which threatens the very stability of the country itself and the region as a whole.

The point of the cuts was to remake the Greek economy, erasing decades of corruption and graft, and to reduce the national deficit and debt. But it is a painful process that Greece's international lenders—other European Union member states and the International Monetary Fund—are demanding happen very quickly, in exchange for regular payments from the European Union's taxpayers to keep the country running, as it is no longer able to attract money from investors. That's right: so that Greece wouldn't default on its payments to investors who bought government bonds, taxpayers are on the hook today and have to pay for the risks of default tomorrow. Essentially, the government has prioritized outside investors over its people. Economists say the risk of another default is high. And as Greece keeps missing lower deficit targets due to hampered growth as a result of the reforms, the requests for more cuts just keep coming. Many ask if this cycle will ever end.

"I feel that what's happening now to our generation is totally unfair. We were raised as citizens of Europe. We are well educated. We are talented. It seems that our ability to contribute to Greece is going to be severely limited," said Alexandra Sigala. "What's so tragic about this generation is we are politically aware . . . but it's kind of futile."

She is 29 and lives in Athens. When Alexandra looks around her, she sees that one out of every three shops is shuttered. About twelve hundred people are losing their jobs each week in a small country of eleven million. She sees well-dressed people who don't seem like they were raised poor but have lost their job and home since the crisis and now survive by rifling through garbage bins for food. "Athens is not a happy city anymore," says Alexandra. "It's driving me crazy, because it's unfair. The people that did not create it are the people that are paying for it."

Her friends are searching for work at half their salary compared to just a year ago. "They were used to some sort of lifestyle, some independence . . . and the competition is crazy because so many people are out of work," says Alexandra. She knows of those also moving back to the countryside, some even turning to subsistence farming. Aristotle University of Thessaloniki announced it would rent small plots of land out to people in need, so they can grow their own fruits and vegetables.

Still, she knows she is one of the lucky ones. Alexandra is well educated. She has a master's degree in media from the London School of Economics and a second master's in political science from Columbia University. She attended the top private school in Athens as a child. She has a job she likes at Marfin Investment Group, buying and managing advertisements for the Greek investment bank. She has had it good in many ways, and the world should be her oyster for the taking. But the view from Athens, even for someone like Alexandra, is bleak. Since the Greek government started implementing austerity measures, she has taken a 10 percent cut to her salary, and her take-home monthly income has decreased another 5 percent due to higher taxes. On top of that, utility prices, including electricity and gas costs, in Athens have increased substantially. She is considering moving back in with her parents.

Vassilis Giannikopoulos has taken to the streets in protest. He is no political activist or an anarchist, as some claim the Greek protesters to be. He's just another Greek citizen, 32 years old and filled with disappointment.

"I went to this demonstration because I wanted to say that I don't like this austerity program, because I don't think it's something that is good for our country. It's only for the banks, not for the people," said Vassilis.

Before he joined the crowd, organizers advised him to wear a mask to protect his face from tear gas, sneakers so he can run, and to completely cover his body with clothes to protect against aggressive police activity. The violence has come from both sides of the police line, though. Protesters have set buildings on fire and looted businesses in an outpouring of hostility aimed at the government's responsibility in the crisis and the way it is handling its consequences.

"I'm not hopeful. I think there is no future here," said Vassilis, who adds that colleagues who have already emigrated from Athens are now making quadruple their Greek salary. "They say our national debt will still be 120 percent of our gross domestic product in 2020 after all this austerity. And until then, it's eight years. What will we do for eight years? We will be in a depression, and what? It's the hardest for young people."

There is an expression in Greek, he said: "The sins of parents make trouble for children." Greece had been spending beyond its means for years and years, addicted to debt and using its membership in the European Union to behave as if it had the finances of its stronger members, even cheating on its budget reports so as not to have to make budget decisions that would make the government unpopular with the electorate. As happens with any addict, life has caught up with Greece.

Vassilis's salary from pharmaceutical company Astra-Zeneca has been reduced and he is experiencing the same tax and price of living increases as Alexandra. But the public services those taxes are supposed to support, such as transportation, are not improving—or even working properly. In fact, most of the country seems on pause, just waiting for word on the next piece of bad news, the next pay cut, the next tax hike.

About a one-hour drive from Athens, Fanis Spanos makes his home in the northern municipality of Chalki. As is customary for many in Greece, Fanis, 27, went into the family business. Small businesses are the backbone of the Greek economy. The Spanos clan makes and sells apartment blocks and concrete. Or at least they used to. Fanis is the third generation to work in the business, and started right after studying engineering in the Democritus University of Thrace. It was 2007 and Europe's economy was doing great. The Spanos business was flourishing, operating with a 30 to 40 percent profit margin. Land in Greece was overpriced. The construction industry made easy money. Fanis thought a master's degree in business administration would help him run and grow the company even more. He received his degree from the Alba Graduate Business School, and his father gave him the keys to the company. It was 2010, and the world was a very different place than it had been when he entered school.

"The whole company's total priorities changed," says

Fanis. "Expansion and big profits were not anymore the main target. All this gave way to strict crisis management."

Clients disappeared. Many who bought concrete lost public sector funding and could no longer pay their bills or make new orders. Demand for land development or new apartments dried up as unemployment rose and wages shrank. The company earns about 80 percent less than in 2008 and it employs about half as many people. This is how government cuts trickle down to the private sector.

"Now I'm very reluctant in investing money in Greece—in buying the land or building the property, or even concrete. I hesitate to purchase new equipment or in general to expand. I am focused on becoming smaller and more efficient," he said. This is a bad sign not only for the Spanos family's business but for the whole country: this risk-averse behavior, as businesses around the country are just waiting for the other shoe to drop, is what's undercutting hope of a recovery in Greece. For instance, instead of buying and building large apartment blocks independently with the business's money, as the company once did, it now only builds on someone else's contract, mostly small private residences. In a sign of the lack of confidence in investing, the company has constructed just four houses in the last year.

"What we used to call a ready-made business, now it's called a commitment," said Fanis.

"Most of my friends from Athens, my classmates, are now abroad. Most of my friends from Chalki that used to work in Athens or big cities, most of them now came back and live with their parents and try to find jobs here or live off of farming the land," he added.

Fanis dreams about moving to Russia or some far-off, faster-growing country. Many Greeks are looking for sanctuary abroad with no intent of returning home. According to the World Bank, 1.21 million Greeks left the country in 2010. That is about 11 percent of the population.

"I think it's hell on earth. Your mind cannot understand how a country that organized the Olympic Games in 2004 and only seven years ago was flourishing all of a sudden just burst," said Myrto Zacharof.

Myrto's family came from meager upbringings. Her father's family fled from Turkey to northern Greece in 1922, but her father rose to become a supreme court judge. Her mother came from a small town in southern Greece. Specializing in Greek history, she worked for a school, where she rose up the ranks, eventually serving as its vice president.

"My parents really believed in education and that if you don't have a big fortune you can create your own by studying," said Myrto. And she once believed that too. But today, at 30 years old, she has a very different view of the world. In Greece, people are very depressed, anxious, and angry. They're pinching pennies in all ways possible, including when it comes to the basics of electricity, heating, and groceries. "There is no positivity anywhere. You can't be positive when you know your company has promised to lay off hundreds of people," said Myrto.

The first university degree is free in Greece, so most young people are educated. As a result, the competition has become tougher than ever as the number of jobs shrink. "You feel you're replaceable, especially because people are just agreeing to ridiculously low salaries," said

Myrto. "People are definitely overqualified for the jobs they are doing."

But Myrto said the crisis was just the tipping point. For young people in Greece, finding stable work has been a long-running problem, due to an inflexible labor market marred by corruption and favoritism. Back in 2004, when she graduated from Technologiko Ekpaideutiko Idrima in Athens with a degree in medical laboratory studies, she fought for a job as a salesperson in a bookstore. She thought more education might help her chances of getting a job closer to her field. So she went to get a master's degree in chemical engineering at the University of Wales in Swansea, after which she returned to Athens, only to end up working at the same bookstore. Her title: retail assistant. She ordered books and organized the warehouse. She was paid €520 per month, about $680. Myrto saved by living with her aunt and grandfather, but something had to give. She didn't have enough money to pick up and leave, so Myrto applied for scholarships and won a grant to enroll in a PhD program in chemical engineering back at Swansea. She studied remotely from Greece and managed to find a job as a part-time teacher. It was around this time that the economy turned for the worse. Myrto was supposed to earn €13 per hour, or about $17, but the state school never actually paid her. Like many others since the crisis, Myrto simply never received the money her employer owed her.

"There were literally no jobs. I just wanted to become a chemical engineer," she said. "I was willing to compromise for a job that paid less to stay in Athens." That's especially because during this period she met her future husband; however, he was in no better financial shape. He had worked cutting and installing tile and marble for residences, but since the housing collapse in 2009, his business had lost 85 percent to 90 percent of its customers. It became impossible for the couple to become financially independent.

"I was expecting to have a couple of kids by now. The crisis delayed that. You're so depressed because you don't have a job. You live on the support of your relatives. You feel so bad that you don't even have the courage to have a sexual life. You're not even dreaming of having children. You don't even have the courage to mate with your partner," said Myrto.

She and her husband decided it was time to leave for good.

Myrto's adviser at Swansea told her about a job opening for a research officer at the university. She sold all her jewelry and some gold coins her family had saved from World War II, giving her airfare and enough money to settle into her new home. Now she is researching ways to harvest energy out of agricultural and waste products. "They pay me what I'm entitled to be paid. It's really interesting and it's very challenging scientifically," she said. Myrto is also considering opening her own business, a nonalcoholic brewery.

"I don't want to go back to Greece. I just want to try my best to earn as much money as possible, because I'm sure that my family is going to need the financial support. We send them money and we try to give them hope," said Myrto.

Her friend Anastasia Tsilimidou took Myrto's advice and left Greece at the end of September 2011. She had worked for a pharmaceutical company as a salesperson. But the company Anastasia worked for was getting squeezed on all ends as the price of medicine kept getting cut and the doctors and state hospitals stopped paying their bills. At the same time, the corporate tax rate was increased.

"I knew that if I would be fired it would be impossible to find another job because the unemployment is outrageous now in Greece . . . you just see homeless people sleeping in streets," said Anastasia. She moved in with Myrto in Wales and found a job a few months later in Birmingham, England, in the marketing department of a firm that researches cancer in plasma cells. She's heard word that her old coworkers have seen their salaries cut by 20 percent, and is glad she is not one of them.

But austerity measures have followed her to the United Kingdom.

Record Youth Joblessness Hits United Kingdom

The United Kingdom government has instituted the harshest cuts to public sector jobs and welfare in more than half a century. It says such cuts are necessary to prevent investors from losing confidence in the United Kingdom, the way they did with Greece. While the British economy is stronger, the consequences for young people have been potent.

The immediate impact, as in Spain and Greece, is weak growth, low wages, and the highest unemployment rate for youth on record, above 20 percent. In the longer term, youth have years of stagnant household income to look forward to—more than a decade without any increase in living standards for those in the middle class, according to the Institute for Fiscal Studies, an influential British think tank. The institute also estimates that total public spending on education in the United Kingdom will fall by over 13 percent between 2010 and 2015—the largest cut in education spending over any four-year period since at least the 1950s. As a result, the United Kingdom is increasingly at risk of too many young people becoming NEET. *NEET* is an acronym for "not in education, employment, or training." In England, they number about one million, or one out of every six 16-to-24-year-olds in the country. And the OECD says the United Kingdom's proportion of young people not in education and unemployed is among the highest of the advanced countries, amid low enrollment in work-study programs and as education spending as a share of GDP is below the OECD average.[6] In 2010, the proportion of UK NEETs grew to 14.3 percent from 13 percent in 2009 and 11.6 percent in 1999. That is above the 2010 European Union average of 11.4 percent.[7]

Steve Martin knows all about NEETs. He has been a jobs counselor for decades in the United Kingdom and recently opened up his own consultancy after being laid off by the government due to budget cuts. The government has closed up training and counseling offices in the country as part of the austerity measures. "We used to knock on [NEETs'] doors, try to recruit them and engage them. That of course is not being done now," said Steve. "Now, surprise surprise, there are more young NEETs."

He adds, "The biggest issue has been the lack of support for people. Colleges have lost staff. Counselors, support staff, people who helped students—a lot of those are gone."

The government moved career guidance responsibilities from its national service to schools, but schools are not actually required by the government to provide the services and don't receive additional funding for them. So even while guidance services are more important than ever in the post-crisis economy, government cuts have made them less available.

"Massive changes are happening very, very quickly," said Steve, alluding to additional headwinds facing Generation Y in the United Kingdom.

Unpaid internships, common in the United States, are spreading in the United Kingdom and becoming increasingly competitive positions. At the same time as jobs that pay are becoming harder to come by, families and students are going into debt for the first time ever to pay for college education, after the government reduced subsidies to universities and raised the amount they are allowed to charge students to make up the difference. Many are unprepared with the necessary savings. Student debt levels are projected to rise to about $83,000 in 2012, double the previous year, as unemployment is expected to remain high.[8]

This has shifted the attitude among the young people Steve works with. They don't expect to ever be able to own a home. They don't expect to have their own pension. Steve advises them to look for more flexible forms of income and not count on a continuous stream throughout their life. But the situation has left many dejected. One disadvantaged 16-year-old boy says the budget cuts have sabotaged his aspirations: "It has become my dream to join the army as soon as I can, but with these cuts there are far less jobs available for new recruits. And my chances of entry are becoming smaller and smaller," he said. The boy's family has been affected too. They live far from the nearest town, and with rising prices for oil and food, as well as higher tax rates on those items because of austerity, even driving out to buy groceries costs more and more. "The financial crisis has forced me and my friends to seriously reconsider our future," he said. For instance, the government closed its Education Maintenance Allowance (EMA) in 2011, which provided financial support for schooling to families most in need. "With the scrapping of EMAs, I will have to find a job somehow to pay for expenses. Before the crisis I expected to get a part-time job somewhere and to be able to use the EMA to help me in further education. I am worried about my future; it is just becoming too difficult."

He is part of a growing group of disaffected youth, a number of whom are protesting their government's seeming disregard for their generation's future prospects. London saw protests by union members against austerity and by young people against university tuition hikes in 2011, but it did not change the government's course. The rage poured over onto Facebook, with a chain posting in November: "Remember when teachers, civil servants, ambulance staff, nurses, midwives, doctors and firefighters crashed the stock market, wiped out banks, took billions in bonuses and paid no tax? No, me neither. Please copy and paste to status for 24 hours to show your support against the government's latest attack on pensions and public sector workers."

Spyro Kokkinakis has been leading the call for an end to austerity in Occupy marches in London, ever since he lost his job as a result of budget cuts.

After graduating from the London School of Economics with a master's in media studies, he soon found a communications job on a short-term contract at a government organization he really liked, the Audit Commission, which was responsible for improving the efficiency of local governments.

"There was potential for me to become permanent there and progress," said Spyro.

But in the summer of 2010, the United Kingdom government shut down the Audit Commission to save money and transferred the functions of the body mostly to the private sector. Spyro was disheartened, but he was able to find a low-level communications job at the United Kingdom Treasury under Chancellor George Osborne, the man spearheading budget cuts. Spyro helped policy makers shape their initiatives for public consumption.

"The last project I worked on, which completely put me off, was the pensions reform. I was talking to the policy people working on this report, and they said, 'What we actually say is people have to work longer and receive less money after they retire, but this is not how we're going to have people see it. Instead, this is a more fair way of distributing pensions.' But wouldn't that be misleading?" said Spyro, who soon after quit.

Many high-level policy experts are stepping out to agree with Spyro and others his age across Europe, advising governments that austerity now—or at least austerity that is this aggressive—comes at too high a price, with damaging consequences for young people and these nations' futures. Instead, they say, the United Kingdom and other countries should increase resources for students and education, including more targeted vocational programs; boost investment in infrastructure projects that could create jobs and improve a country's roads or transportation networks; and lower tax rates for already stressed groups, as well as reduce their child care costs. In addition, Europe should focus on opening up the borders inside the continent to allow workers to move more freely to where work is available, and be able to transfer accumulated benefits with them.

Only 3 percent of Europeans live in a country in Europe where they were not born, because of the disincentives to move. Migrants from outside of Europe make up a larger 5 percent.[9] To make this policy effective, countries have to recognize the professional qualifications of neighboring states. Leaders should also focus on boosting a single European market, which could increase access to funding and customers for small businesses. Many efforts thus far have been paralyzed by national pride.

David Blanchflower, who used to advise the interest rate policy-setting committee at the Bank of England, suggested higher government debt in the United Kingdom would even be worth it if the government could create jobs.

"Moves to cut public expenditure as suggested by some political groups, deep in a recession are a mistake. The danger is that they will turn a recession into a depression," he wrote in a paper with David N. F. Bell, a budget adviser to the finance committee of the Scottish Parliament.[10]

While some alternative initiatives are gaining momentum in Europe, a lot of damage has already been done. At a conference of leading academics and policy makers in Brussels, Belgium, Sir Anthony Atkinson, a leading British figure on inequality studies who has been writing on the topic since the late 1960s, told the attentive room: "Whatever you thought was the right amount to leave to your grandchildren, you should give them more."

3

Breaking It Down: The Labor Market Is Rigged Against Generation Y

Good habits formed at youth make all the difference.
—Aristotle

Labor markets around the world were already stacked against young people heading into the crisis. They have been pushed into temporary contracts or precarious internships, told these are the only options to enter the workplace, and sucked into a cycle of low-paying jobs. The American dream grows further out of reach. Now, after the crisis, it's even worse.

Liz Guidone, 22, has been caught in the unpaid and low-paid internship trap, despite graduating from Millikin University in Decatur, Illinois, with a degree in music business in 2011. She's had four unpaid positions, mostly organizing details for events and retrieving hot cups of coffee. For one company, she was asked to vacuum the 9,000-square-foot office at least twice a day, wash dishes, and wipe down desks. In return she received a college credit, which she paid for, and her employers offered her no training or field experience. In essence, her employer wanted a college student to be their maid so that they wouldn't have to pay anyone. After Liz's schooling, she worked at a public relations firm for $10 per day, but ended up in the hole because she paid $600 per month just to commute to work, since she couldn't afford to rent an apartment near her office on that salary. Like many 20-somethings, Liz is willing to work hard for very little in order to gain experience, but her employers aren't giving her the training she needs to get ahead. None sought to retain Liz as a full-time employee after her internship ended. They just went on to the next free or low-paid Millennial worker. Meanwhile, Liz and others like her get stuck in the no-man's-land of the labor market.

"After my last one, I am through with internships. No matter how exciting or educational the internship, I find it insulting to be an unpaid intern as a college graduate," she said. "It seems like it's the only position we can get, even though we voluntarily became thousands of dollars in debt for college tuition."

Liz decided to move back in with her parents in Madison, Connecticut. She is now employed as a full-time receptionist at a spa near their home.

"Life sucks at the moment," she said.

This is not what it was supposed to be like.

The number of 20-to-24-year-olds working less than thirty-six hours per week in part-time positions because of economic reasons—meaning they would like to work full-time but either have had their hours reduced by their employers or have been unable to find full-time jobs—has more than doubled in the United States in the past decade and is at its highest level on record, as firms increasingly rely on flexible labor contracts to cut costs. However, this statistic doesn't even take into account all the Millennials working unpaid or internship positions for economic reasons, or those who are paid "off the books" with a small sum in cash. The United States Bureau of Labor Statistics does not regularly document these types of posts, but their inclusion undoubtedly would increase the number significantly.

In the past, political and industry leaders, as well as colleges, often encouraged part-time or temporary positions as good experience or resume fillers, particularly during periods of low employment, arguing they can lead to full-time jobs. In 2011, for example, President Barack Obama proposed a program that would let businesses temporarily hire young workers without having to pay them directly. Instead, the government would pay them unemployment insurance or a small sum of money, with the hope that the employers might eventually hire a worker full-time.

But temporary jobs are not turning into plum, full-time posts. To the contrary, temporary and part-time jobs can set a lower bar for Generation Y's income indefinitely. People just keep moving from one post to the next, failing to find stability.

"We find no evidence that temporary-help placements provide a port of entry into stable employment," new research by Massachusetts Institute of Technology economist David Autor and Susan Houseman, a senior economist at the W. E. Upjohn Institute for Employment Research, shows.[1]

They compared the prospects over a four-year period of more than thirty-seven thousand people placed in either temporary jobs or regular contract positions by a Detroit welfare-to-work program called Work First, and discovered that temporary placements actually diminished participants' subsequent earnings and employment outcomes.

"Rather than helping participants transition to direct-hire [or regular] jobs, temporary-help placements initially lead to more employment in the temporary-help sector, which serves to crowd out direct-hire employment," said the study.

In other words, the study showed that this program reinforced an unstable work model of job hopping and unsustainably low pay, and allowed employers to continue hiring people at generally lower wages, rather than offering employees full-time jobs with benefits. More broadly, this is evident in the jobs created in the United States since the Great Recession as well. A large portion of the modest increase in job numbers that we've seen in America in recent years are temporary positions replacing once-permanent posts, introducing a higher level of instability into the American economy and Generation Y's future. Those on temporary contracts are regularly paid less than their full-time counterparts, even if they perform similar functions and have the same experience.

Other terms of employment in these non-regular jobs are systematically worse than standard employment too. That's because the social protection net—benefits and insurance—in the United States is directly tied to the employer. If the employer doesn't hire the worker as a standard employee, the employer doesn't have to make contributions to social security, unemployment insurance, workers' compensation, or health insurance. Employers will also save the administrative expense of withholding taxes, and aren't even responsible to the worker under labor and employment laws. Obviously, if the employer doesn't pay into the system, the employee doesn't get any of these benefits, nor is the employee legally entitled to sick days, vacation, or severance. Young people have been the most vulnerable in this system and are statistically the most likely to be stuck in these unfavorable jobs—people like Geoff Beitscher, 29. Geoff has been moving between temporary job contracts and paid internships since getting laid off from a full-time job two years ago. The posts are mainly administrative and tied to business school classes he's started taking at Rider University, hoping a master's degree will help his prospects. But because the jobs are tied to class credits, Geoff actually pays to work. Not only is Geoff using some of his savings to pay for school in order to work, but he receives no benefits and pays for health insurance out of pocket. He is accepting of the situation—he didn't expect to receive any insurance in this economy or work environment.

Part of the reason Generation Y is most vulnerable to the short-term job trap stems from the simple paucity of jobs for college graduates, due to the fields they are studying in, crowding out by the baby boomer generation, and budget cuts that have reduced the number of jobs available.

The United States is now set to produce twice as many graduates in the social sciences and business than in science, technology, engineering, and mathematics—a trend that could leave the country with a nearly two-million-person shortfall for technical and analytical positions.[2] Indeed, while a "good liberal arts education" is considered the backbone of the United States college education, by pursuing this track Generation Y is missing out on jobs just waiting to be filled because they haven't been informed about the jobs available at the end of their schooling and the needs of the United States economy.

Compounding the situation, there is also an increasing number of older workers staying in their positions for longer. The financial crisis has reduced their savings, lowered the value of their stock portfolios, and slashed the selling price of their homes. The money in the bank is inadequate. Now their outlook for retirement has been pushed back. Nearly four out of ten adults working past 62 years of age say they have delayed retirement because of the recession, and workers between 50 and 56 years old say they will also retire later than expected. Plus, with people living longer, healthier, and more active lives, many baby boomers don't even want to retire as early as workers did in the past. That's left fewer openings for a new generation of workers, at the same time as companies are employing fewer people in an effort to increase profit margins. (Indeed, this corporate trend, coupled with lower salaries, pushed United States companies' profit margins to an all-time high in 2012, even as individuals were still suffering in the wake of the crisis.)[3] Now the government estimates that 93 percent of the growth in the labor force from 2006 to 2016 will be among workers age 55 and older, as the participation rate for this age group in the workforce is at its highest level in fifteen years, crowding out people between 16 and 24 years old, who currently make up their lowest share of the workforce since 1948.

Budget cuts since the crisis have exacerbated the situation as well. They have led to the starkest cut in public sector jobs at the state and local government levels since 1955. But the crisis has stripped confidence from the private sector employers too, undercutting job creation outside government. Moreover, overall, 95 percent of all the net job losses during the recession were in middle-class jobs, which offered Millennials entry into the workforce.[4]

Look at the field of education. "Because of all the budget cuts there are hardly any jobs in public schools unless you do extra schooling for special education, which is more stress, time, and money," said Laurel Lederman, who just finished her master's degree in education at the Bank Street College of Education in New York. "Since the job market is so competitive now, there are probably ten thousand people just like me fighting for the same jobs, making it nearly impossible to be truly qualified."

For now, she is working as an assistant kindergarten teacher at a charter school in Harlem, but the job is secure for only two years and she's eager to find a classroom she can lead on her own. Most starting salaries for teaching jobs are below $30,000 per year, she added.

"That is not enough to live on, and over the years I've accrued almost $6,000 in credit card debt and had to move back home [with her parents], where I currently live," said Laurel.

But given expectations for government and businesses to remain financially strained for years to come, it is unlikely the United States will be able to create the twenty-one million jobs needed to return to full employment—work for those who have lost their jobs and making room for new entrants—sometime this decade.[5]

The other part of the reason rests with government, which shoulders a lot of the blame for the rigged labor market against Generation Y. Weakening labor laws have allowed employers to hire new workers with more flexible contracts, including part-time and temporary positions. The United States Bureau of Labor Statistics says companies taking advantage of short-term contract worker schemes by misclassifying employees as not full-time employees, even though they are performing the jobs of a full-time worker, is a "growing problem," as it denies workers access to critical benefits and protections, such as family and medical leave, overtime compensation, minimum wage pay, and unemployment benefits. Researchers at the Global Union Research Network say that the "calculated regulatory evasion" of labor laws by employers in the United States to push people on temporary or irregular contracts is unparalleled among the developed countries—and it's today's young workers who are hit hardest. The researchers credit the United States' employer-based social protection system, which makes it expensive for bosses to hire full-time workers, as well as a litigious business culture, which has seen the development of legal specialists to advise employers on how to dodge requirements.[6]

There have been warning signs for years, even public government reports, showing that certain laws encourage employers to shirk standards meant to protect their employees.

In 1994, the United States government put together the Commission on the Future of Worker-Management Relations to publish a report on the status of the American worker, who spends more time at the workplace than the citizens of any other advanced country except Japan. It concluded that tax, labor, and employment laws give employers incentives to hire workers on a contingent basis—independent contractors, temporary workers, subcontracted and leased workers, and part-time workers—"in order to evade their legal obligations" to support workers with certain benefits and job security.

"Congress and the [National Labor Relations Board] should remove the incentives that now exist for firms to use variations in corporate form to avoid responsibility for the people who do their work," the commission advised.

More than ten years later, in 2006, there had been no meaningful change in labor laws on this front, and the United States Government Accountability Office reported that these contingent workers remained a relatively constant percentage of the working population, about 31 percent.[7]

And now the situation has become all the more unstable for new entrants into the workforce, as young workers struggle to find permanent positions amid an economic crisis in a system that is already unlikely to favor young workers with stable jobs.

The consequences of this discriminatory work structure are already clear. According to the Pew Research Center, the net worth of a typical household headed by an adult under the age of 35 has declined dramatically since 1984, by 68 percent to be exact.

In this way, the crisis has laid bare a long-bubbling problem in the United States labor market. And if the United States doesn't correct the system, the problems could become truly entrenched for young people, as in the cases of Italy and Japan. Already the United States shares many of their characteristics.

Italy and Japan's Second-Class Citizens: Lessons for the United States

In Italy today, nine out of ten people's first jobs are temporary contracts, no matter the level of education. Most Italians' twenties and thirties are spent in low-salary temporary positions, moving from one six-to-twelve-month contract to another, in a society dominated by tradition and old men in both business and politics. Some are even on rolling contracts that need to be renewed every month, putting young people constantly at risk of losing their job, while older workers enjoy regular positions.

In 2003, legislative reforms introduced short-term contracts in Italy. They were part of an effort to bring more flexibility into the labor market and increase the employment rate, and were spearheaded by government economic adviser Marco Biagi, who was assassinated outside his home in Bologna for his work on these policies just months before their implementation. Previously, employers had been forced to give workers a no-termination agreement after three years of employment, making it virtually impossible in Italy to fire a worker with a permanent contract. If fired, workers could sue for wrongful termination and judges would force employers to rehire them. Those who were hired before 2003 still have these old contracts, though, while a whole class of young new workers has next to no protection. As a result, the labor market has grown segmented, where the older workers have it relatively good and the young have it relatively bad. Workers employed on the new flexible contracts can't even qualify for unemployment benefits if an employer decides not to renew their short-term contract. Young people are completely unprotected. Across the continent, many countries have a similar problem, where old codes in place create very high hurdles to both hiring and firing employees. That's led employers to utilize new temporary contracts, like those in Italy, that take advantage of young workers.

Millennial Italian Eleonora Maria is just one of thousands

of examples. A passionate scientist with a master's degree in biotechnology, Eleonora wants to use her background to write about advances in the field. She worked for one firm on a short-term internship, in another as a maternity-leave replacement for one year, and elsewhere on back-to-back six-month temporary work contracts. She moved from place to place in search of just one employer who would allow her to work permanently and pursue her ambition.

"I think I was a dreamer—not a good thing in these years," said Eleonora.

In her last position, she was a copywriter for a health care communications company, Sudler & Hennessey, and earned €750 per month. She calls the job a tease. Her boss promised her a full-time copywriter job at the end of a second contract, but instead the company decided not to even renew her temporary status for another half year. She has no recourse. Now she feels used and unvalued—and angry.

"They promised me a role that does not exist. I wish that they were just honest. The result is that in the hope of making a good career, I lost one year."

She is ashamed that she has to live in her family's home near Lake Como. It's difficult to talk over the problems with friends, even though most are in the same position. She feels that her life is on hold. She is 30, but it seems like life is stuck at 24. The only people she knows in stable jobs are those who entered the workplace before labor market reforms in 2003. "I would like that my parents are proud of me, but I'm 'a problem.'"

Her expectations for the future aren't any better: "Less salary, less security at work, less independence."

This system has produced a generation of nonstandard workers, whose precarious position in the labor market—indeed, whose precarious future—has become even more uncertain in light of the crisis.[8] For instance, Marta Vassanelli is a 27-year-old architecture graduate from the University of Venice who is on her second short-term contract at a firm in Trento, Italy. For two months before finally giving her a second contract, the firm wouldn't pay her amid uncertain economic conditions in Italy. They promised Marta that a second contract was coming as long as she stuck around while they figured out how to weather the crisis. When her checks do arrive, Marta gets paid €1,100 per month, about $1,400. On paper, as a temporary worker, she's only supposed to work on one project: restoring Lavis-Giardino dei Ciucioi, an ancient garden and church. But she's often juggling multiple projects at once and stays at the office working late hours on whatever drafting project her boss needs done, working well beyond the limits of a temporary contract.

"In other offices here in Italy, conditions are similar, and you have to work even more hours. Some friends of mine in Milan work for bigger offices and are paid the same, or less. We have no insurance, no health days, no holidays," said Marta. "I think that it's like saying to people that your work doesn't have any value. And it's not really true. I am in the office every day, and I know it's important to them. But all the people my age have this situation in Italy."

"Unemployment is only a secondary problem here. The first problem is the way you work," she added.

At first, Biagi's reforms appeared effective. The unemployment rate for young people steadily declined. But it was a sham: young people were working, but in positions that offered little in the way of opportunity or protection. Among people between 25 and 34 years old, short-term contracts rose from 14 percent in 2004 to 17 percent in 2008, and for 19-to-24-year-olds the figure rose even more.[9] This led to a deterioration in starting salaries, ultimately making young people second-class earners.[10] It also became increasingly difficult for young Italians to build a career network of strong connections in their field or garner valuable experience, since they are always in transition, leaving them ill-equipped to find a permanent position, especially after the crisis wiped out so many jobs. This is why the effects of the crisis were felt on Italy's labor market so much more strongly than in many other countries in the European Union. Generation Y was employed in unstable positions that employers shed fast and first. The youth unemployment rate in Italy rose from 20 percent in 2007 to above 30 percent in 2011. This also contributed to the growth of job overqualification, which means young people are wasting their college education and years spent in internships on positions meant for people with much less experience. In 2009, more than one million more individuals were overqualified for their work than in 2004, especially university graduates between 24 and 34 years old, according to the National Institute of Statistics in Italy, said Professor Annalisa Murgia of the University of Trento, an expert in the field.

The rise of temporary job contracts is also contributing to an increase of poverty among workers. Temporary contracts on average carry a 14 percent wage penalty relative to permanent jobs, a penalty that impacts a worker's salary at each consequent job for years. Moreover, mobility between temporary contracts and permanent contract jobs is not high, according to the European Commission, which compiles assessments of the European Union's economies.

This means that low-wage, transient work can become a persistent feature of a person's working life. For instance, the OECD found that many training and employment programs are reserved for the unemployed or require full-time participation, which means that someone with a part-time or transient job can't benefit. Potential new employers might also view applicants with a background in temporary work as uncommitted and unlikely to have deep knowledge or training in a particular field. This could make temporary work a dead-end destination, when it's supposed to be just a starting point. That's why nearly everyone accepts the temporary contract as a last resort. More than 90 percent of temporary employees say that they accepted a fixed-term contract because they could not find a permanent contract.[11]

This instability has lowered Generation Y's probability of building a family in a society already suffering from low birth rates, which weighs down economic growth as well. It has also diminished reasons to attain a higher education. Just 20 percent of Italians between 30 and 34 years old hold a university degree, well below the European Union average of 35 percent.[12] More than 20 percent of people between the ages of 15 and 29 neither work nor study.[13] It's little surprise that almost one-third of Italians live with their parents well into their thirties.

Italy is now making efforts to reform the economic divide facing Generation Y, but most economists agree that proposals are modest and it will take a long time to see their effects. Instead of waiting around for jobs that have not materialized, many are choosing to move abroad, following the advice of people like Massimo Fantini. Eight years ago, when Massimo was 26 years old and studying for his certified public accountant degree in Milan, temporary work was just becoming common in Italy. Massimo's degree required work experience, and he was forced to take on an unpaid internship.

"I was working for a certified public accountant, and he was asking me to follow him around, just for people to see me, in order to get exposure. And he was saying, 'You must be happy I'm introducing you to all these people.' Like, I should be grateful I was working for him and he wasn't paying me, only for the connections," said Massimo.

Seeking a more merit-based system, Massimo moved to New York through a university-supported six-month job placement program. He never returned. He is now married to another new New Yorker, a woman who left China in 2000, and lives in Greenpoint, Brooklyn. Back in his homeland, though, he saw that others were not so fortunate, and their luck spiraled lower after the crisis struck. "After three years, they simply do not renew agreements with these employees," said Massimo. "It's difficult for young people to have a long-term job . . . and in the crisis now, companies took advantage."

This led Massimo to cofound Professionisti Italiani New York City, an association that helps Italian professionals make the same move he did. While many people who reach out to him want to come to America, the economic landscape in the United States leads many of them to inquire about moving Australia. "They just want to run away," said Massimo.

However, Valeria Mura is one Generation Y member trying to make the best of it, and keeps herself busy studying, working, and dreaming. She has always wanted to become a diplomat for Italy. She loves languages and traveling, and wants to serve her country. She graduated from the University of Turin in 2007 with a major in international studies and went on to a two-year course to build a specialty in international relations and the protection of human rights. She continued her education further and was accepted into a competitive program to study Chinese politics and culture for two weeks. She kept searching for work during all this time but ended up just accepting one unpaid internship after another.

Thinking the capital city might offer more opportunities, she decided to follow her boyfriend to Rome. The relationship didn't last, but she stayed and rented a room in an apartment with three other people for €490 per month. Housing in Rome is notoriously expensive. Her parents help her. "I don't like it at 27 years old, but I have to."

In the beginning, she says, she sent out almost five hundred resumes over the course of six months. She applied to be a personal assistant, for anything related to international relations, and for jobs that could make use of her knowledge of languages. Besides Italian, she knows English, French, German, and some Mandarin. Then her search grew wider, to almost anything available that she might qualify for. All of the positions were temporary contracts, and nearly all of them were unpaid at least for the first several months. Rarely did any of the jobs offer security beyond ten months.

She received a few responses, and even scored some interviews. But no jobs. Part of the problem was due to the large pool of applicants. Part of the problem was just the Italian system, where merit is often not valued as much as having someone owe you a favor or knowing an applicant's parent. She also received responses that read: "Thank you, but for us you are too well-experienced to be an intern, and you don't have enough experience to work for us." Valeria said it was like "Dante's limbo." At this point, she had been working as an unpaid intern for eight years.

She finally accepted a two-month unpaid internship at Vatican Radio. The alternative would have been to do as many friends did and move back home, maybe work at a café. But the post opened a door to a job related to her field. She then won an unpaid four-month contract to work at the Italian embassy to the Holy See, the jurisdiction over Vatican City. She helped organize events. After the term of the contract was up, though, they offered not a full-time job but another temporary contract. She accepted. They did that six times, short-term contract after short-term contract. The embassy at least started to pay her a "decent" wage, says Valeria—only about €1,000 per month, which is roughly $1,300. But she worked about forty hours per week, the hours of a full-time job.

"Compared with my parents, it's totally different. Even if you never attended university, it wasn't a problem to get a job," she said. "Now it's different because a degree is the new basic level. And then after the crisis, yes, I think is more difficult to find a job. The crisis worsened a system already unbalanced."

Japan's history offers another chilling example of where the United States may be headed without a drastic change of course.

In the late 1980s and early 1990s, Japan experienced an asset price bubble like the United States' latest, when real estate and stock prices rose beyond their value. The bubble popped and Japan's economy crashed, along with the job outlook for young people. New entrants to the labor market during this period, as well as other young and vulnerable workers, were pushed into irregular positions, leaving a whole class of underemployed people in unfair work contracts. In the beginning, staying out of the workplace or finding a part-time position was actually thought to be a conscious choice among some Japanese young people, a sign of rebelling against the traditional one-company-for-life tradition. But it soon became clear that many young people didn't even have the option of accepting a regular position. The so-called Freeter movement was born—people under 35 years of age who graduated from school but are either completely out of work, are searching for their next temporary job, or currently have a part-time or temporary work status. Receiving low salaries with few prospects for advancement, these young workers experienced the same hardships troubling young American workers today. Cultural hurdles in Japan made the fallout even worse, because companies typically hire new employees right out of college, or even before they graduate. The longer a graduate is out of work or in temporary positions, the less attractive he or she becomes to Japanese companies, which prioritize loyalty. So the longer it takes for a graduate to get hired, the less likely it is that he or she will ever be able to secure a stable job. Years after the onset of Japan's crisis, many of these now not-so-young workers are still stuck in unfavorable temporary posts. Their situation has been slow to improve— both because they now find it more difficult to maintain a full-time job after years of temporary work and because employers distrust their ability after being unable to secure anything but temporary work. Their number peaked in 2003, eclipsing 2 million, and has remained around the same level ever since.[14]

Chiyoko Hirakawa, now 36 years old, has experienced the changing work model firsthand. It has been more than ten years since she graduated from Nagasaki Junior College with a degree in English-language studies and got her first job on a nonpermanent contract with Fukuoka City as a public employee. After her third year of work, the city wouldn't renew her contract. That introduction to the labor market affected the rest of her working life, impacting the way she saw her role in the workplace. She had to learn to adapt to temporality in her career, and it became so that the full-time jobs she eventually secured felt overwhelming. Chiyoko found a regular contract job producing concerts and other events in Japan and abroad, but the work was too much for her. The job was extremely hectic. She was required to work late nights regularly and had no time to take vacations. Chiyoko didn't want to do it anymore. She quit. Now Chiyoko is back to doing "desk work" in a temporary job at the Fukuoka office of a Nagasaki-based television station on a rolling six-month contract. She helps companies place commercial advertisements on the station's broadcasts but has little interest in the field of work. Still, she says she would prefer a permanent job because of its predictable payments and job security. "That kind of job [regular contract work] provides a proper and determined salary you can expect every month. . . . My current job as a dispatched worker is based only on an hourly wage with no bonuses. It's about the working conditions, you see?" she said. And as Chiyoko gets older, she anticipates that her prospects for finding better work will diminish. "I'd say that I have little hope at this point."

The consequences of Japan's crisis in the 1990s are now impacting the next generation of workers too, in a sign that post-crisis labor market stress is truly lasting. Employers continue to take advantage of irregular employment options, a narrow avenue of flexibility in an otherwise heavily regulated and relatively well-paying labor market. After the latest global economic crisis, the shrinkage of traditional employment paths has meant that more and more young men and women are entering into temporary or part-time contracts, not by choice but by necessity. Employers are differentiating between those who were there pre-crisis and those who started post-crisis, and treating them accordingly in pay and benefits. In 2010, almost half of 15-to-24-year-old workers were still getting stuck in non-regular jobs, compared to 17 percent in 1988. Moreover, a record low of 57 percent of upcoming graduates had job offers at the end of 2010.[15] Permanent workers in Japan, with benefits and job security, are mostly above 40 years old. This leaves the entire young workforce economically insecure, which became abundantly clear recently: hundreds of thousands of non-regular workers' contracts were allowed to expire, underscoring the low value attributed to the young workforce.[16] To make matters worse, the country is facing the additional struggle of overcoming the economic turmoil left by an earthquake and tsunami in 2011. And until very recently, government has largely ignored these threats facing Generation Y and Generation X, even though the phenomenon is widely acknowledged. In fact, this problem facing Japan's younger generations is even being parodied in video games. One of game developer e-smile's latest role-playing projects is called Ore-ni Hata-rakette Iwaretemo, or How Can You Ask Me to Work. The lead character is someone not in employment, education, or training. The young man's parents die, and he then has to find ways to pay his own way.[17]

The instability of Japan's workforce seeps into other areas of the economy too—a reality that the United States appears set to follow. For one, Japan's shrinking workforce has to shoulder the burden of paying for a population that has aged significantly since the 1990s, just as the United States population is set to age in the years ahead. Second, young workers are competing with middle-aged people for jobs, and more often than not are losing out.[18] This is contributing to a growing risk: the failure to transfer skills to younger workers, which could undermine economic productivity in a country that has to correct massively overleveraged accounts. Japan's public debt is double the size of the $5 trillion economy. Once the second-largest economy in the world after the United States, it has since fallen behind China and is expected to soon fall behind India. All of this should sound familiar to those worried about the United States' position in the world.

"You could think of the trends in Japan as possibly the shape of things to come in Europe and North America," said Andy Furlong, a professor of social inclusion at the University of Glasgow, who has researched the situation in Japan.

"Like Japan, the initiatives taken in Europe and the United States to overcome the precarious position of young people are destined to fail because they are all based on the idea that the root of the problem is a deficit of labor supply. In reality, the problem is there are not enough jobs or the right type of jobs for the young and educated workforce," said Furlong. "New jobs in Japan, and in the movement we're seeing in the United States, often require little in the way of skills and are based on precarious forms of working."

For instance, in the United States, two-thirds of occupations projected to have the largest number of new jobs over the next decade will require less than a post-secondary education, no related work experience, and short- or moderate-term on-the-job training. These lower-skilled jobs will, obviously, also be lower-paying jobs—pushing the American dream further away.[19]

This illuminates the ultimate question, not only for Japan but also for America and elsewhere: if young people are underutilized now, why would they stick around, hoping for things to get better later? Many aren't.

4

Expectations Crushed, Young Leave Ireland: A Warning as United States Brain Drain Risk Mounts

Forty-four percent of Millennials have confidence in the United States federal government's ability to solve problems, compared to fifty-five percent of people between the ages of 18 and 32 a decade ago—a full eleven percentage points fewer.

—Center for American Progress, "The Generation Gap on Government," July 2010

More than half of young adults in America say they don't have enough money to lead the kind of life they want.

—Pew Research Center, March 2012

There are few places where Generation Y's expectations have been so dramatically overturned in the aftermath of the crisis as in Ireland. As a result, many of the nation's young are packing up and leaving—a pattern that is a threat in many of the world's advanced economies.

Take a look at *Ireland's Lost Wall*, a website launched by Dubliner Colin Hart that is a living memorial to those who have left Ireland with the hope that they'll soon return. The website says: "This wall is a reminder for us not to forget the people who are emigrating and so that we can strive to make Ireland a place for them to want to come back to."

Émigrés can add their own names to the site and write about why they fled. The most common reason is the lack of employment opportunities. Darragh O'Connell, now in Melbourne, Australia, summed up the general feeling in his posting on the website: "I've left to find real opportunities that will allow me to reach my full potential."

It's Saint Patrick's Day in 2012, a usually happy and party-filled commemoration of the country's patron, but Adrian Collins, 26, is sitting at home with his parents. In past years, he might have gone to the parade or hit up some bars in Dublin to celebrate. He doesn't feel like it this year. He's not missing out on much of a party anyway. Most of his friends are at home with their parents too—they are nearly all out of work and without much money to spare. A €5 beer is just too expensive. And the mood is glum in much of the city, which has seen a lot of changes in just a few years.

The standard of living has declined. You don't see as many designer clothes or fancy cars on the streets of the capital as you once did. You don't see as many people either. Ireland's total population is only around 4.5 million people, and about 50,000 emigrated in 2011, with at least the same expected in 2012.[1] Before the economic bust, between 13,000 and 15,000 Irish nationals emigrated each year. However, the unemployment rate remains the highest in decades, despite the shrinking pool of competition. Near Adrian's family house in Dundrum, a complex of luxury apartments built around Ireland's biggest shopping center sits half finished. Other high-end buildings appear to be completed, but no one is living inside them.

It's a hard pill for Adrian's generation to swallow.

"It's all people are thinking about all of the time," he said. "The crisis."

This is a stark turnaround for Ireland and its economy. Adrian grew up during what is known as the Celtic Tiger years, between 1995 and 2007, days of fast economic growth and a high-flying real estate market. Prices just kept rising, but jobs were plentiful and salaries rose too. Those who warned it was all just a bubble waiting to burst were quickly shushed, even by the prime minister:

"Sitting on the sidelines or on the fence, cribbing and moaning, is a lost opportunity. In fact, I don't know how people who engage in that don't commit suicide," said Irish prime minister Bertie Ahern in 2007, to laughs and claps, mocking the cautious.

Many really believed Ireland would never again see crisis, after experiencing decades of terrible suffering until the 1960s and then again in the 1970s and 1980s. After all, it had bounced back strongly into the 1990s, when Ireland boasted about its nearly free college tuition, ensuring highly skilled workers into the next century. Ireland also has one of the only growing populations in Europe due to high birthrates and a low corporate tax rate that attracts many big companies, such as Google—a combination that set the country up for success.

But the housing market did sink in 2008, after the United States housing market collapse, driving the banks that made loans to homeowners and builders to the brink of bankruptcy. The government promised to protect the banks and their account holders—it would bail them out. As a result, little more than a year later, the government no longer had enough money to service its own expenses. Trade was shrinking due to the global crisis. Ireland was broke, and leaning on investors. For many, it was déjà vu. For young people, it was unbelievable that a pattern their parents said should never happen again was now affecting them. There have been cuts in education and research funding (which led Ireland's leading universities to drop in global rankings), a lack of jobs, and few options but to move abroad—repeating the exits of their parents in the 1970s and 1980s.

Adrian has felt the consequences firsthand. He studied Spanish at University College Dublin for his bachelor's and master's degrees and was encouraged by his professor to continue in 2008 for a doctorate. He chose to research Argentine writer Jorge Luis Borges. Funding was already strained, but he was able to teach a few classes to support his research.

By his second year in the doctoral program, though, research funding sustained additional cuts. In the first semester, he received enough money to teach just one class. In the next semester, Adrian's funding was completely cut. He had to leave the doctoral program at University College Dublin.

Adrian wants to be a teacher, to build lesson plans, create curriculums, and educate students. He saw his pursuit of Spanish—the world's second-fastest-growing language—as a real boon to his country, which has a poor history of teaching foreign languages. Sadly, ever since the budget cuts started, a government initiative to introduce languages in primary schools was abandoned.

"I won't be going back there," said Adrian. "I definitely want to finish the PhD. I know I probably won't be able to finish it in Ireland."

In this way, Adrian, a PhD candidate from a middle-class

family, whose father was a diplomat in the country's foreign service, ended up working at a local sports shop, selling soccer balls and team shirts—and was grateful for the paid job, as many peers wallowed in the country's recession.

By 2010, Ireland's crisis had spiraled further. Economic growth stalled and the youth unemployment rate mounted to near 30 percent, three times the pre-financial-crisis level. Ireland could no longer find investors willing to buy its bonds at reasonable rates. They feared the country would default on its payments—Ireland was already relying on the European Central Bank to support the nation's major financial institutions. In turn, though, the ability of the government to make those debt payments diminished, as did its ability to pay the country's teachers and hospitals, or even put garbage trucks on the road. Like most countries, Ireland relies on investors to lend it money to keep its government running. Some argue Ireland should have held out, but as its crisis threatened economic stability in neighboring countries, European Union members pushed the government to accept an emergency funding program. Ireland would receive about $90 billion over the course of three years from the European Union and the International Monetary Fund. However, the terms of the rescue were harsh and the money was promised on the condition that Ireland meet certain economic targets that officials from outside the country would regularly check up on. The government had to cut wages, slash work hours, increase taxes, and decrease federal spending all around. Ireland is now in its fourth consecutive year of elevated tax rates and reduced government spending—a formula that's led the country into another recession. The reforms are supposed to make Ireland more competitive in the future, by, for example, reducing the government's reliance on debt or decreasing the cost to employ workers. Yet in practice, as we've seen around the world, the country's economic growth remains weak, and the outlook for the future is equally grim. Local businesses, hurt by increased taxes and by fewer customers, are suffering or being shuttered. Teachers and some other government workers saw salaries cut in half, but their mortgage payments didn't change. So while the country was already roiling from the immediate shocks of crisis, it was now flagging under the hand of austerity measures.

It's hardly surprising, then, that since 2005 migration out of Ireland has doubled, with most of the emigrants between the ages of 20 and 35—the same people who benefitted from Ireland's drive to provide a valuable education at a cheap price to all. When such a significant portion of an area's skilled labor force leaves for a more favorable place, it is called a brain drain. This is Ireland's biggest brain drain since at least the 1980s, and some say it may be the biggest wave of emigration since Ireland's last famine in the 1800s.

Adrian thought he would try leaving too. He applied to teach English at a secondary school in Zaragoza, which sits between Barcelona and Madrid in the northeast of Spain. It was a part-time job that he hoped would give him time to do the research to complete his doctorate. But it wasn't financially viable for him to live off the €700-per-month salary, less than $1,000, so he taught additional courses in the evenings. As a result, he ended up with only about an hour and a half of spare time each day, which he spent preparing for all the lessons. His PhD kept moving further out of reach.

So Adrian returned to Ireland.

Now he's registered at eleven different recruitment

agencies that help him search for jobs. He's sent applications to Google, Twitter, the University of Madrid, Apple, and others. He even sat for a video interview with Apple, but with so many people out of work, the competition is incredibly high. The company hired someone before Adrian was even done with the interview.

"I never expected to be some super-rich person. I was hoping I would at least not still be living at home," said Adrian. He has set a deadline for himself: if in a few months he can't find a place at a university overseas that will fund his degree, he's giving up for at least a couple of years and will try to find work somewhere else in the world.

"There is a whole generation that knows we're not going to be in Ireland for the next ten to fifteen years," said Adrian.

Molly Muldoon is one of those who have found a home outside Ireland since the crisis, and she feels thankful.

She is also 26 years old and now lives in the Astoria section of Queens, New York. She moved in September 2009, after losing her job and seeing the landscape in Ireland change.

"In our generation, growing up in the Celtic Tiger, we only saw the dizzying heights of a really strong economy. . . . To have that shift in expectation, it is quite strange," said Molly. She remembers working in a bar throughout college and getting paid an hourly salary of €10.25. At the time, she didn't think much of it. Now, six years later, she'd be pretty happy receiving a wage like that in Dublin.

She and three of her classmates moved into a house together after graduating.

"The rent was great. It was a beautiful house. We all thought we were going to be there for a few years," said Molly. But within just a few months, two out of the four housemates were laid off, including Molly. She had worked as a researcher for a news radio station, and they let her go just two months into her contract, when advertising revenues and government funding dropped dramatically.

"I was devastated. I worked hard to get that job and I enjoyed it, and I thought it was the start of a bright future at the company," said Molly. She and her roommates all ended up working sporadically, freelancing on various projects that year, or claiming social welfare when nothing came their way.

"At the end of the year, one of the girls moved back home to save money, another girl did the same, and me and my other friend, we both emigrated," she said. "Everything had changed so drastically."

But "you just get on with it," says Molly. That's the Irish way. She recounted a story about an unemployed construction worker who subsequently trained as a baker and now employs other people. Life moves on.

She is happy in New York. She has lots of friends who relocated there from Ireland, and she works in her field, which she probably wouldn't have been able to do at home. She is the deputy editor of the website Irish Central and a reporter for the *Irish Voice* newspaper. She knows that things have gotten worse at home, and there is a consensus among the young Irish people she hangs out with in New York that they're not returning anytime soon.

"I don't think it would be a wise move because of the prospects," said Molly. Still, she misses her family and friends, and gets sad thinking about the nieces and nephews she doesn't get to see grow up. When her grandfather died this year, she couldn't go to the funeral because she had just recently paid for a trip to visit.

"There is a good chance if I had never lost my job that I would still be in Dublin," she said.

Many of the young who are leaving Ireland do not want to. They want to follow through on the life they were promised, and live in and contribute to their own country. It's just becoming harder to see how this is possible anymore.

Sharon Hickey tried relocating to Australia after she was laid off in 2008 from her job in television journalism. "After reaching Australia, I had the initial euphoric 'grass is greener' feeling about the place," she said.

Australia doubled the number of visas granted to people from Ireland between 2010 and 2011. Visas to Canada, New Zealand, and the United States also increased dramatically since the crisis.

But Sharon felt like a second-class citizen, an outsider and unwanted. She wasn't home, and she thought she would have to settle for a job such as working at a bar, waiting tables, or answering phones at a call center.

"The jobs that nobody else wanted," as Sharon says. "I decided that it wasn't for me."

She landed back in Dublin about twenty-six weeks after she had left. She searched for work for five months and finally found a job on a very popular television show as a researcher. But then Sharon was laid off again. At this point she is 27 years old and experiencing a very bumpy start to her career. She freelances for two television shows and is interviewing for a permanent job.

"I really wish that the responsibility to pay off exorbitant loans didn't fall on my young shoulders," she said. But Sharon feels worse for Ireland's more recent graduates.

"If I were to stop and think of the injustice, the closed

doors, and the uphill struggle that faces the 21-year-olds of 2012, I wouldn't be able to get up out of bed any morning. It grieves me to think of what young graduates in my industry must be feeling right now. Their parents must be at their wits' end. It's just an endless cycle. It shouldn't be like this," says Sharon.

Conor Kirwan is one of those recent graduates. He has been looking for stable work for more than a year since graduating from Ireland's Trinity College with a degree in history and political science. He lives with his parents less than twenty miles outside of Dublin in the town of Bray.

His father works for a transport company, and his mom is an administrative assistant—"decent stable stuff," says Conor. These days, he's relying on them a lot more than he'd like to. The only job Conor could find with his degree is at a wine shop.

"This is not what I spent four years in college for," said Conor. "It's not an ideal situation. It's not what I expected at this age."

While in school, Conor was mostly independent. He lived in an apartment with three others and worked as a restaurant manager, waiting on tables, or tutoring high school students.

He didn't have high hopes of finding a real, permanent job after university, since the crisis was well under way. "It wasn't about finding the dream job. It was about paying the bills," said Conor. He was open to accepting an internship in Ireland, anything to keep his resume growing and gain some experience, but he just wasn't getting any replies.

"I examined my resume many times. I had it looked at by other people. Most of the feedback I was getting is

I've got a very decent resume, but there just isn't a huge amount out there for anyone," said Conor. He has been proactive and attended career fairs. But at the latest fair, the participants were promoting work visas to go to Australia, rather than opportunities in Ireland. Conor doesn't want to leave his home. Most of his friends who have stayed in Ireland are just like him, working in positions they are overqualified for. Friends who trained to be teachers are all out of work, because the state has stopped hiring. Some are luckier, especially those who graduated with degrees in computers or another specialized area. But it seems like more and more people he knows are leaving the country. For instance, some who worked in construction management and couldn't get an interview in two years have left for Australia. Out of his high school class of about 140 people, 35 have already moved abroad for work. About half of his class from Trinity has left. To be sure, many are just looking for an adventure, but it's not like they have much choice in the matter. The goal for most university graduates isn't to just find a working job. It's to start a career and a lifetime of opportunities. Two of the four people in his university apartment have also skipped town—one to Italy and one to Germany.

"They want to start their careers. They want to have their future, and they can't see that future starting here. At the same time, it's almost like people are saying let's give up. But if there were enough staying or making a lot of noise, somebody might actually pay a little more attention to the problem," said Conor. "I want to point to the prime minister and say, 'I'm staying at home and you better do something about it.'"

His family expects Conor will eventually go too. It is a constant topic of conversation at the dinner table. The talk quickly becomes painful for everyone.

"I find myself getting quite emotional about it," he said.

Conor is especially sad about his best friend, an environmental scientist, who found better options in New Zealand.

"These are real people. They are not just numbers and statistics," he said.

This flight of talent out of Ireland is something his parents have seen before: "They really thought it would never happen again, with the coming of the Celtic Tiger and Ireland achieving so much," he said.

The mood before the crisis was "Today is good, and tomorrow will be even better."

Conor had a lot of hope for his future. "Now the feeling is tomorrow is going to be worse—more job losses, state finances are getting worse," said Conor. "All that growing-up stuff . . . they're all becoming a more distant future. Everything is paused right now in terms of my life, except that I'm getting older.

"Somehow we failed, but this really shouldn't be happening," he added.

The exodus and the fragility of the economy have angered many in Ireland, who say taxpayers are unfairly footing the bill for banks and their owners. A small community in Ballyhea, which has about a thousand inhabitants, has taken to the streets to make their message clear. Every Sunday for more than a year, local residents march from their church down the major highway and back, sometimes joined by groups from other towns, politicians, or noted economists who come to lend their support. The marchers' major concern is the future of their children.

"The odd thing about our protest here is that it is comprised mostly of the most unlikely candidates for protest. Most of us are middle-aged, a few pensioners, many others young parents, all worried about the future for our own kids," said Diarmuid O'Flynn, an organizer of the march and a sports journalist at the *Irish Examiner*.

In the end, a country that has produced a highly educated and skilled population could merely become a source of talent for other countries. Ireland loses out on its investment and its future. It misses out on taxes and revenues from these potential workers too, which it so desperately needs, extending the time horizon for Ireland's economic recovery. Young people are left bitter and under pressure, searching for an opportunity promised and carrying the lower-wage effects of early unemployment with them.

The Lesson for the United States

Like Ireland, the United States will need to make aggressive reforms to its economic policies to correct a bulging deficit. The long-term hope is that it will improve the nation's global competitiveness. But as people see what's happened in Ireland under the axe of austerity, and as economic opportunities inside the United States shift, some are getting the cue and taking off.

For the first time ever, the United States is now on the losing end of a brain drain. The crisis has seen the country's status in the world decline, and as businesses reap greater rewards in the developing world, the United States is surrendering its competitive edge: the educated innovator.

While it is hard to come by precise data, since the United States government does not track and publish the movements of its citizens, the Department of State has estimated that the number of adult American citizens overseas increased from 3.8 million in 1999 to 6.4 million in 2011. It has also reported an increasing number of children born to United States parents abroad, especially in Asia—a sign that many are settling into their new homes and putting down roots.

Surveys by America Wave, Inc., a company that studies where Americans are moving, break down the trend further. They show that young people who were born in the United States are now increasingly thinking about moving abroad. In a survey of households conducted just before the financial crisis, an average of 1.4 percent of respondents planned to relocate abroad. In a subsequent survey in 2011, the total rose to 2.5 percent, closing in on three million households and six million people. Generation Y accounted for the biggest jump. Nearly 40 percent of survey respondents between 18 and 24 years old have turned their minds toward leaving the United States, whether or not they can afford it right now; in 2007, that figure was only about 15 percent. The figure for the 25-to-34-year-old group also increased to about 5 percent from less than 1 percent in 2009. Some of these young people might just be looking for adventure and a chance to explore the world. But a growing number are deciding to stay in emerging markets to work and build businesses.

Rich Yang immigrated to the United States as a child with his parents from Taiwan.

"We definitely had the American dream," says Rich.

His father didn't speak a word of English but managed

to open a restaurant, succeed, and send two children to expensive universities.

Rich attended Pepperdine, and moved on to work at Deloitte Touche Tohmatsu Limited, one of the largest professional services firms, for eight years. But he wanted to start his own business. Looking around, he was more excited by opportunities happening outside the United States and was enticed by adventure.

He applied for business schools abroad, and when the financial crisis hit in 2008, he felt his decision to go to IE Business School in Madrid was validated.

"I'm glad that I'm leaving here and getting to see the world from a different perspective," Rich thought at the time.

After school, he first moved to Singapore to launch a film festival, finding sponsors and negotiating royalties. It didn't work out, and he closed it down with his partner six months later. They moved back to New York to restrategize and think of new ideas. Still, the attraction to stay in the United States was dim. They applied to start-up incubators, which help companies launch their business, but a program in Chile offered him more than United States programs. The Chilean program invested $40,000 in the company and didn't require an equity stake.

"The Chilean government had put this program together to foster and spur innovation in Chile," said Rich. He didn't see anything else like it closer to home. In Chile, Rich started to build the idea around a travel guide website that eventually became Street Mosaic. After the program, he moved to Brazil, which he saw as the perfect place to launch a tourism business.

"The opportunity now is in Latin America," he said.

Clint Nelson, who cofounded Startup Labs, is not surprised by this sentiment. He helps early-stage technology companies develop in emerging markets, and U.S.-educated or -born entrepreneurs are often behind them.

"I think it's just kind of the path of least resistance," said Clint. People move where there are greater opportunities. That's it. No longer is the United States seen as *the* land for opportunities for Americans.

But that's not the end of the outflow from the United States. High-skilled entrepreneurs from India and China who were studying or working in the United States are leaving by the tens of thousands each year, attracted by better economic and professional opportunities in their home countries, according to research by the Ewing Marion Kauffman Foundation, which promotes entrepreneurship in the United States. These immigrants have historically been important contributors to the American economy, a group that often stays in the country for the long haul and creates jobs and wealth. They are more likely to create companies that produce high-technology and high-paying jobs, which the United States needs now more than ever to get ahead.[2]

"Most returnees now say the entrepreneurial advantages are better in their home countries, where they can benefit from lower operating costs, heightened professional recognition, greater access to local markets and a better quality of life than they could attain in the United States," says the Kaufman Foundation. In a survey it conducted of 153 Indian returnees and 111 Chinese returnee entrepreneurs, respondents said these opportunities play the biggest role in their decision making to leave the United States, even more than the expiration of their work or study visas. Only 14 percent of Indian respondents and 5 percent of Chinese respondents said that opportunities had been better in the United States. This reflects the growing dynamism of certain fast-growing emerging market countries too, not just a simple goal of leaving the United States. However, the longer economic growth, wages, and academic and business funding remain under pressure, the more time other countries have to narrow previous opportunity gaps with the United States and attract talent that used to be pulled by its shores. And the timing is not good. Population growth data signal that over the next few decades, the majority of the United States' labor force growth will increasingly rely on these immigrants and their children to fill vacancies left by an aging population.

Ricky Sperber is a perfect example. He moved to the United States in 1999 from Ecuador to study finance and international business at the University of Virginia in Charlottesville. Many of his classmates made the move to attend school in the United States, as there were few educational options closer to home that provided a degree of equal quality. (This is no longer the case: Ricky's younger brother and his classmates now largely go to college in Argentina.)

Ricky was in no rush to go back home after graduating. He got a job with Merrill Lynch in Miami, looking at investment opportunities in Latin America. He stayed there for nearly a year, and then studied for the Chartered Financial Analyst exam. He moved on to a position with BBR Partners in New York, a wealth management firm, and stayed for three years, helping to determine and allocate investments for clients. His interest in finance evolved, and he decided to take a job at Citi doing research on Latin American bank stocks. He started in January 2008, right before the big market crash. Because of the health of the Latin American economies during the crisis, his job was secure. Ricky was happy to be living in New York. By now he was 27 and had spent nearly a decade in the United States.

Then 2010 came. His work visa was about to expire, and Citi couldn't renew it.

"Because they laid off so many United States workers, the government wasn't allowing Citibank to sponsor any workers from abroad," said Ricky. It quickly became clear he couldn't stay. Citi decided to move Ricky into its Brazil offices to do the same work from there, and he could reapply for a visa to return to work in New York after a year. All along, though, he had been thinking about using his background to start a business, and now he worried that this move might delay him.

Ricky arrived in São Paulo in January 2011. He settled in, and after about two months he went on a short getaway to El Salvador for Carnival, the annual festival before Lent. In the airport he met the regional heads of Groupon, the global Internet company that sells local discounts for services. They partied at Carnival together and kept in touch. "They're telling me about e-commerce in Brazil. In my mind, I couldn't grasp this growth and opportunity they're talking about," said Ricky. "I was so surprised."

As Ricky learned more about electronic commerce in Brazil, it became a very exciting idea to him. He finally found his opportunity to become an entrepreneur. He quit his job at Citi and, at 30 years old, with an education and business experience from the United States, took action in Brazil, where the opportunity to thrive appeared far greater. He teamed up with an architect and an interior decorator to launch an online retailer for high-end home decorations, called Design Outside the Box.

Now it doesn't even cross his mind to return to the United States.

"What am I going to do there? It's going to be very tough to find a job in finance," he said. "Because of the crisis, they didn't extend my visa or give me residence. Because I came to Brazil, I ended up opening a business in Brazil and not in the United States. . . . I see a much lower risk of my business not doing well here in Brazil than in New York, because of the state of the United States economy, and especially because the Internet here in Brazil has a very big tailwind."

Bikui Chen is another example. He hails from Chongqing, China, and after studying at Tsinghua University in Beijing for his bachelor's degree in engineering, he went for his master of science at the Massachusetts Institute of Technology. When Bikui graduated, he stayed in Massachusetts and worked at Oracle Corporation, leading a team that developed Web-based applications for clients such as the Swiss financial services giant UBS and the United States Department of Homeland Security. At the same time, Bikui started his own company, the short-lived Privasource Inc., which developed software that helped health care companies comply with patient privacy laws. But opportunities in the United States grew boring, and the chance for more money and exciting business opportunities seemed far better on the other side of the world.

"There are just way too many things that we could have done in Beijing or Shanghai than in the United States, and

I am also a single man—easy to move from city to city," he said. He decided to leave and got a job in Shenzhen as the special assistant to the chief executive of Shenzhen Development Bank.

"That's the kind of opportunity I will never get in the United States," he said. Working side by side with a chief executive at a leading bank in America is a learning experience many business schools students would probably pay for.

When Bikui decided to go back to the Massachusetts Institute of Technology for a second master's degree in business administration, he completed it and then moved back to China immediately and started his own business in Shanghai. (Despite seeing more promise for work abroad, Bikui and most others agree that the most valuable education is still in the United States.) The start-up is focused on luxury online retail for Chinese shoppers, a fast-growing market that doesn't face as much competition as in the United States.

The United States is at risk of damaging its global competitiveness by not making a greater effort to hold on to these entrepreneurs at a moment when the country needs the job creation and innovation they can foster. Noncitizens hold about one-quarter of all international patent applications in the United States.[3]

Brain drain is also spreading to other important sectors of the economy. The number of doctoral degree recipients in the sciences and engineering planning to stay in the United States on temporary visas is, for the first time in a decade, on the decline, according to the National Science Board. Just before the crisis, these numbers peaked. The National Science Board says the United States is simply contending with many more significant international competitors than ever before—competitors who are prioritizing funding for and education in the sciences.

"Not long ago, one fought hard to come to the United States to pursue graduate education and then to stay. I know; I did. . . . We may be witnessing the beginning of a potentially rapid shift," said Subra Suresh, director of the National Science Foundation, in a speech in 2011. He says the United States could lose out if it doesn't increase basic research expenditures to around 3 percent of GDP from about 2 percent.[4]

Dr. Suresh received his first degree at the Indian Institute of Technology Madras in 1977. In his graduating class, more than 80 percent of the 250 engineering students had the opportunity to pursue graduate studies in the United States, and nearly all of them took it—and all of those remained in the United States, becoming citizens or permanent residents and contributing to the country's research, industry, or business sectors. On a recent visit back to his alma mater, he discovered that more than 80 percent of the latest graduating class had the same opportunity to go to the United States, but only 16 percent accepted.

"And it's not the top 16 percent," he said.

While the number of people exiting the United States in search of greater opportunities remain relatively muted, especially compared to Ireland, it should be seen as an early warning of what is possible as America's luster continues to fade.

5

The View from the New
Promised Lands

I'm not going to surrender to other countries the technological leads that can end up determining whether we're building that in this country. So we're going to have to keep on pushing hard to make sure the manufacturing is located here, new businesses are located here and new technologies are developed here.

—United States president Barack Obama, October 2011

Those jobs aren't coming back.

—Steve Jobs, the late cofounder and chief executive of Apple, to President Barack Obama at a dinner with leaders in technology in 2011, when asked why Apple doesn't manufacture its products in the United States[1]

Opportunities for young people in emerging countries have flourished over the past decade, but after the crisis, these nations are providing more advantages than ever before. Emerging markets, such as China and Brazil, offer a haven for jobs and hope in an otherwise floundering global economy. In an international survey of more than one thousand people about the outlook for their economies, 64 percent of respondents in China and 62 percent in Brazil assessed their country's current economic situation as good, compared with 22 percent in Belgium (an open economy that can often be seen as a gauge for the European Union as a whole), 21 percent in the United States, 13 percent in Great Britain, and 6 percent in France.[2]

It's easy to understand these attitudes. When the crisis hit the United States and Europe hard, Generation Y in Brazil benefitted from an economic growth rate of more than 7 percent after a brief recession. In China, growth eclipsed 10 percent. However, both countries' growth has since slowed as the crisis in the advanced countries began to impact the developing world. By comparison, the growth rate in the United States has been stuck around 3 percent, and in Europe it declined. The consequence is that China closed in on Japan and finally beat out its neighbor to become the second-largest economy in the world, after the United States. Although Germany and France follow in fourth and fifth places, respectively, Brazil also made a significant move, outflanking the United Kingdom for sixth place. Indeed, Brazil, Russia, India, and China—the largest developing economies—are on track to account for 70 percent of global economic growth in just the next few years and will surpass the developed world's share of global GDP.[3]

Faster growth has allowed these countries to invest in their economies and people in ways the United States and Europe have not, particularly since the crisis. Now more and more members of Generation Y in emerging markets are gaining a higher education, helping their nations become strong global competitors and boosting the outlook for their futures. In China, for instance, the proportion of the population with a college education has almost doubled in the past thirty years from 3 percent to about 6 percent. As a result, the United States and its advanced-economy peers are falling behind in education—what has been their most important edge. Between 2003 and 2011, the European Union, the United States, and Japan lost a combined thirty-two spots to emerging economies on the list of the top five hundred universities produced by the Academic Ranking of World Universities. During this period, China more than doubled the number of its universities that made the ranking, from nine to twenty-three, while Brazilian schools increased from four to seven. Expenditures for higher education, as well as research and development, are especially increasing in emerging economies, while it has increased proportionally much less in the United States. For young people, stronger national growth also translates into a stronger job market. On top of expanding domestic businesses in emerging markets, more and more big United States companies are seeking to access those countries' higher economic growth and educated populations by creating more jobs in the developing world, especially in the fields of technology and science. After all, that's where the talent which companies need is becoming concentrated: more than half of the world's engineering degrees are awarded in Asia, as opposed to just 4 percent in the United States, and many of that 4 percent are immigrants.[4] Today, workers in Brazil, Russia, India, and China, the so-called BRIC countries (a term coined by Goldman Sachs to single out these nations' growing economic might), already make up nearly half of the world's labor force—and are quickly moving into the middle class, raising the prospects of Generation Y.

This is why new entrants into the BRIC workforces are met by optimism rather than fading expectations. The middle classes in Brazil and China are on the rise, rather than under attack, as perceived by many in the United States. It is estimated that more than thirty million people entered the middle class in Brazil over the past decade, making the middle class now more than 50 percent of its population.[5] While China's middle class constitutes a smaller portion of its huge population, closer to just 20 percent, it is growing. In contrast, the OECD predicts that North America's share of the global middle class will shrink to 7 percent by 2030 from 18 percent in 2009, at the same time as Europe sees its share decline to 14 percent from 36 percent. Meanwhile, countries in the Asia Pacific region, including China, will see their share increase to 66 percent by 2030 from 28 percent in 2009.[6]

As a result, in one of the clearest examples of the changing global landscape, immigration to the United States from Brazil and other high-growth countries has slowed since the crisis. During the first half of the 2000s, immigrants contributed to two-thirds of the total growth of the United States labor force. Since then, the share of labor force growth due to immigrants has dipped to less than half. Even net immigration from Mexico, the source of the United States' largest wave of immigration in history from a single country, came to a standstill after the crisis. It just stopped.[7]

For emerging markets, a bigger portion of the global pie in wealth and workers also means something else for their governments and Millennial-aged population: more power. Developing countries are gaining greater influence at global negotiating tables, lifting their interests and that of their Generation Y citizens higher on the world's agenda. Many members of Generation Y say they have been heartened by the evolving boldness of emerging world leaders, captured in an exchange between Brazil's president, Luiz Inácio Lula da Silva, and British prime minister Gordon Brown in a 2009 press conference, when Lula said: "This crisis was caused by the irrational behavior of white people with blue eyes, who before the crisis appeared to know everything and now demonstrate that they know nothing." For many Millennials, this shift inspires pride in their countries and confidence in their future within those borders.

Generation Y no longer sees the American dream as beholden only to American shores. This presents a mounting risk to the traditional dominance of the United States and its peers in providing opportunities for future generations. Developing countries are not only attracting American-educated entrepreneurs, as discussed in Chapter 4, but retaining top home-bred talent—a group of people that once sought to better their chances in the United States or Europe.

This chapter focuses on Brazil and China in the BRIC block, because of their impressive growth and development. Russia's role in the group and as a global influencer is questionable given the combination of a declining population, worse than expected economic growth, its move toward a more authoritative regime, and regular lack of cooperation on global policy decisions, especially regarding the Middle East. This has led to a surge in emigration from Russia in the last decade. Meanwhile, India still has much further to go in terms of development and faces arguably greater hurdles in overcoming poverty.

Brazilians See Greater Opportunities at Home

"When I was a child, I always dreamed about living in Europe or in the United States, because I used to think that there was 'another world,' an almost perfect world there," said Murilo Ramos Rodrigues de Paula, a graduate school student at Pontifical Catholic University of Rio de Janeiro, one of the top universities in Latin America. In the 1990s, he watched American movies and television shows with admiration. "They depicted the American way of life or the comfortable welfare state in Europe," said Murilo.

At the time, high inflation and reduced government spending were ravaging Brazil's economy. Interest rates rose as high as 45 percent in 1999. The government tried to counter the crisis by devaluing Brazil's currency, which meant that the buying power of the Brazilian real diminished from one day to the next. Some people's wealth disappeared overnight. This crisis hit the rest of Latin America as well, and it took years for the region to recover.

However, Brazil learned from its mistakes, and in the time between its financial crisis and the Great Recession implemented significant reforms that strengthened the country's economy and allowed it to weather the latest storm better than the economies of the world's richest nations. The government adopted an inflation target that has helped Brazil sustain lower real interest rates than in the past. It also lowered fiscal deficits over time, so that it would not have to make dramatic budget cuts and tax hikes in the middle of a downturn, by setting clear rules on the administration of public resources and mostly sticking to them, even when times were good. These included limiting public debt, defining annual fiscal goals, and instituting controls on spending ahead of an election. Brazil also built up international reserves that insulated the economy during the heights of the global downturn, when investment slowed. Brazil increased oversight of its banking sector, reducing the risks financial institutions took that built up to the crisis elsewhere. The International Monetary Fund has praised Brazil for raising transparency and disclosure standards in capital markets and introducing risk-sensitive solvency requirements in the insurance sector. "Brazil's strong financial markets infrastructure and strong regulation and supervision have been an important factor in maintaining financial stability, although there are a few areas that could be strengthened further," the IMF said in a 2012 statement.[8] Since its crisis days, Brazil also diversified its exporting partners, making it less tied to any single industrialized economy, and thus less vulnerable to the downturns in the United States and Europe. Only about 10 percent of Brazil's exports now go to the United States, which after eighty years has lost to China its position as Brazil's top trading partner. Brazil also made strides in recent years to shrink the income gap between the nation's poor and rich with effective public programs, including subsidies that help people purchase their own homes and pay for education, as well as raising the minimum wage.

This combination of policies, and the government's dedication to them, has boosted Brazil's economy and its status in the world. For the first time, Brazil is a major player on the world stage, pushing for emerging economies to have greater deciding powers at Group of 20 meetings since the Great Recession began, and offering its successful responses to past crises as advice to nations currently suffering from economic uncertainty. It has publicly argued for a larger say at the International Monetary Fund and World Bank as well, and hosted the first-ever official meeting of the BRIC finance ministers in 2008 in an effort to forge solidarity among emerging countries so they can together gain more global influence. In 2012, Brazilian finance minister Guido Mantega told Reuters that it was only a matter of time before European countries listened to the advice of the major emerging-market countries: "They will change their strategy and will accept the suggestions made by the BRICS countries to combine fiscal consolidation with economic stimulus," Mantega said, expanding the group of Brazil, Russia, India, and China to include South Africa.[9] Meetings between key emerging-market finance ministers or heads of state continued throughout the crisis and were closely watched by the rest of the world, which has come to depend on these economies.

As a result, now 22 years old, Murilo says his views of the United States and Europe have changed—and so has his view of his home country.

"I think, nowadays, that I can achieve my goals in Brazil," he said.

For people like Murilo, whose father traversed the economic volatility in Brazil to become a cardiologist and can now afford to send his children to seek better opportunities abroad, that is not an insignificant step.

"I am witnessing many changes, like the growing of the middle class, the improvement of the institutional environment and the improvement of social indicators, such as education and health," said Murilo. "The economy and the social environment are changing very fast, and there are lots of opportunities here for people who want to work hard."

In Brazil, the economic boom is palpable. Construction is everywhere—new houses, hotels, and businesses—as private wealth grows. And the demand for construction projects is high. Property prices have skyrocketed: the cost of an apartment in Rio de Janeiro has doubled since the beginning of the Great Recession, when prices sank in most parts of the world. A new transportation network is also in the works ahead of the 2014 World Cup and the 2016 Summer Olympics, events that have reinforced excitement about opportunities in the country. Foreign investment in Brazil keeps beating records, also spurred by valuable oil discoveries off the coast of the states of São Paulo and Rio de Janeiro. Foreign capital inflow to Brazil has grown from $24 billion in 2001 to $137 billion in 2011. Money is outbound from the country too—private outflows totaled $33 billion in 2011—in a sign that the wealth sloshing around Brazil isn't only foreign.[10]

Brazil's strong currency and rising incomes have given local consumers unprecedented abilities to spend at home and abroad and has forged an optimistic Generation Y, as captured by the Brazilian Dream Project, a study of 18-to-24-year-olds through nearly two thousand interviews across the country. The study of what the researchers call "the first global generation of Brazilians" discovered that 76 percent of respondents believe Brazil is changing for the better and 87 percent think it is important in the world today; 25 percent want to chase the profession of their dreams; and 77 percent intend to go to college. Survey respondents defined their generation as dreamers and consumers, responsible and hardworking.

"Nowadays, Brazilians see the United States and Europe with less dreamier eyes than people of my parents' generation used to see these places. It seems that currently, Brazilians started to value more Brazil than they used to in the past," said Murilo.

Eduardo Pinheiro Fraga, a 22-year-old classmate of

Murilo's, is another example of someone who has adjusted his view of the world and his country's place in it since the crisis.

"We saw that unemployment, recession, riots, political crisis, and the like are not exclusive to the poor, but can also happen in the developed world. At the same time, developing countries like Brazil, China, and India managed to maintain reasonable levels of growth during those years, so the situation on the whole contributed to reduce the impression I had of great disparity between rich and poor countries," he said.

"The difference between the average person in Brazil and in the United States may be still really big in terms of income and goods, but is not that great in terms of necessities, fears, hopes, and expectations," Eduardo added.

He was especially affected by a backpacking trip he took in Europe during the crisis in July 2009.

"I had the chance to watch the routine of the people in their daily lives, and many of the issues that affect these countries became evident: marginalized populations, prejudice among ethnic groups, drugs, prostitution, and many other things. That was by far the most important proof that the 'perfect' society I imagined was not really real."

This awakening has been a countrywide phenomenon after the crisis, he said. Brazilians, who have never been that optimistic about the future, are suddenly becoming more positive about their country. As a result, fewer of his peers, some of Brazil's highly educated and trained young, have interest in working abroad for very long, if at all. Those eyeing a career in the private sector, like as an analyst at a bank or as a financial market trader, are interviewing for jobs in Brazil, whereas in the past a post in the

United States or Europe would have been preferred. "The prospect of working abroad relative to working in Brazil is not really attractive," said Eduardo. "There is plenty of opportunity to get fairly good jobs for a post-grad here."

The country's growing financial sector—as well as a strong mining and oil industry and retail sector—has in fact led to a shortage of skilled workers to fill all the jobs the economy is creating. Brazil is advancing faster than its skilled workforce is growing, a development that gives young people like Eduardo and Murilo an advantage—a fate unimaginable in the United States today. Employees in the financial industry in Brazil often jump from bank to bank in pursuit of higher incomes. Defecting Brazilian investment bankers overall received a 25 percent pay increase in 2011, at the same time as New York firms hemorrhaged jobs and cut salaries.[11] In fact, Brazilians are currently earning up to 85 percent more than their counterparts in the United States or Europe because of the labor shortage. Their skill set and education are valued. That's not only encouraged more Brazilians to stay home but also attracted highly educated immigrants the United States might have lured in the past. The largest group of skilled newcomers to Brazil is now coming from Spain, seeking relief from their country's massively high unemployment rates as a result of the crisis.

Lorena Cazares moved to Brazil from the suburbs of Atlanta, Georgia, to be with her Brazilian boyfriend, who after a short-term study program abroad returned home to work in the country's petroleum industry. She decided to take advantage of her time in Rio de Janeiro by pursuing her master's degree in economics.

"It has been a humbling experience to participate in the

revelry here in Brazil thanks to the upswing in the domestic economy while listening to news about several relatives back home who stopped paying mortgages and are waiting in suspense for the banks to come and foreclose on their homes," said Lorena. "I know some people [here] who are already employed before they graduate. . . . It's much more optimistic than in the United States, as far as salary, as far as actually being employed full-time."

But Lorena still wants to go back to the United States: she just doesn't feel comfortable in Brazil.

"I really want to leave. I know the job market is really good. But I don't think the pay is high enough to compensate for living here."

While the Brazilian economy is on the rise, lifting the outlook for Generation Y there, it is still a developing country and has a long way to go to match the quality of life in the United States. Prices in Brazil are high for everything from groceries to rent, despite efforts by the central bank to tame inflation. High taxes play a big role, especially in pushing up the prices of imported goods—Coca-Cola costs more in Rio than in New York. Buying an apartment is more expensive than in the United States, even though salaries are generally lower. The *Economist*'s Big Mac Index, which measures how much a currency is overvalued based on the cost of a McDonald's hamburger, puts Brazil's currency among the most overvalued in the world, below only those of Switzerland, Norway, and Sweden. And although there is this pricey and shiny facet to the economy, it belies a large wage gap within a population still suffering from a significant poverty problem. Brazil's cities are marked with slums. To be sure, the government has reduced economic inequality faster than nearly anywhere else in the world, but Brazil's Gini coefficient—the standard measure of income inequality—is still one of the highest in the world. Its education system is also ranked among the lowest, except for those who can afford expensive private schools, reinforcing the large gap between the rich and the impoverished. As a result, high rates of violence and crime persist, amid a rising illegal drug presence.

For businesses, Brazil poses additional challenges. Office rents in Rio are more expensive even than in New York. To employ someone, companies have to budget not only for an additional salary but also for taxes that often add up to twice the employee's take-home pay. In addition, the World Bank grades Brazil as one of the most difficult countries in which to conduct business. In order to start a business in São Paulo, a company has to check its proposed name with the State Commercial Registry Office and pay a registration fee. Don't lose the receipt for that payment, because you need it to register with the commercial board of the state and obtain an identification number. This will cost about $40. It will then take about twenty-two days to obtain tax numbers, since state authorities have to inspect a company's headquarters before approving registration. You then have to pay a fee to a municipal tax authority of more than $200. It will take a couple of days to apply for and obtain a digital certification for an operations permit, which costs $230, and another day to register all employees with the social integration program, to protect them in case of unemployment. The company has to open an unemployment account in a local bank branch and make regular payments into it, which employees can withdraw from if they are terminated without cause or if they become disabled, among other reasons. Finally, the company finally has to register with the labor union to make sure it is respecting employee labor rights, and it must pay annual fees to the union. For comparison, in the United States, setting up a limited liability company in New York City should take just six days, but it does cost a couple of hundred dollars more.[12]

Additionally, for all the inflow of investment into Brazil, infrastructure and key transportation networks remain unreliable. One of the most common complaints is congestion and traffic in the cities, as higher wealth has led to more cars and more jobs in the center. *Time* magazine called São Paulo the world's worst traffic jam. This has led to the growth of one of the largest helicopter fleets in the world, as rich executives seek faster means to get around. While focus on public transportation networks is increasing, railways remain unreliable and buses are stuck in the same traffic as cars.

Brazil is most definitely improving on all of these fronts, but it is still clearly a country emerging from its past, which is why 19-year-old Yuri Zaidan remains concerned. He launched a gaming company called ICare Games in Porto Digital, a region in the Recife area of Brazil, where technology start-ups often choose to build their home. He says Brazil's favorable points, including high growth, increasing foreign attention, and relative economic stability, are overshadowed for businesses such as his by high federal taxes, which can sap up to one-third of a company's earnings.

"Because of this, a lot of entrepreneurs give up and can't sustain a company," and many foreign investors choose not to support Brazilian start-ups, said Yuri. As a result, "a lot of entrepreneurs see Europe and the United States like the 'land where magic happens.'"

"Even with the economic crisis, it's there that the great

client segments are concentrated, as well as infrastructure, tax breaks, great investment funds. And it's all of this that, in Brazil, we still don't have in abundance," said Yuri. "Even with the consequences of the United States and European crises, these are the places that I long to have my company in three to six years."

Brazilian-born members of Generation Y are honest about their country's shortcomings, but for many, they aren't a strong enough deterrent from staying at home, a new world of opportunity.

Pedro Ernandes Purkyt is in his final year at the University of São Paulo, studying marketing. As a child he had been intent on leaving Brazil as quickly as possible.

"If I really want life quality, of course I would live outside of Brazil. The public services work. You have good transport systems. Here, everything is overcrowded in Brazil, at least in São Paulo. Outside of Brazil, you have good public education. You don't have to hide your stuff in your pockets when you walk on the streets. Here you can be mugged on every corner."

However, the strong, and still strengthening, economy is pulling him to stay.

"If I work hard enough, I can get good money, which in the past wasn't true. I feel like [I'm] in a bubble here in Brazil, because we just see in Greece and Europe, they are really broke and we don't feel that here at all at the moment. I see Brazil getting better and better opportunities over time."

While he finishes his university degree, Pedro has a part-time job at a company that works on advertising videos to play in stores and supermarkets. "It's pretty exciting because it's a really growing market. Now lots of United

States companies are coming to Brazil to do that," he said.

Caio Praes, 23 years old, has similar feelings. He was impressed with the "opulence" in the United States when he attended an American high school in 2005 and 2006, before the financial crisis. Now he sees the United States for what it is.

"My father's secretary leased a BMW, a friend in high school drove a Corvette. The impression was that everything was accessible to everyone—stylish clothing, cars, houses, everything. It didn't make sense to me where all this money was coming from, even though I recall a presentation on how to have a high credit score—maintain frequent small purchases in your credit card—and commercials on the TV directed at Spanish-speaking homeowners. Now I realize that much of this opulence was on credit—in Brazil, if you try to live on credit, you'll be bust in no time—and people I deemed rich may have had negative equity at the time," said Caio.

Eyeing a career in finance, Caio says his best chance for success is in Brazil.

"I believe I can achieve these goals in Brazil. I don't think it would be easier in Europe or the United States . . . When I hear that MBA students are applying for summer jobs in Brazil, I suspect that the prospects here are rosier right now."

Young People in China Still Dream About Freedoms Available in the United States

Generation Y in economic powerhouse China also sees the United States and Europe with new eyes after the financial crisis. Propelled by the fact that China's economy has been even more robust than Brazil in its aftermath, long-held assumptions about the perceived opportunity gap with the West are changing rapidly. The Chinese government has supported consumers with spending programs and kept bank lending open with easy monetary policy, which means the central bank increased the amount of money in financial markets and reduced the threshold commercial banks must hold in cash. As a result, economic growth remained strong during the crisis. Moreover, China's growth during this period probably saved the rest of the world from a sharper falloff in the global economy. Its population of more than one billion people (compared to the United States population of more than 300 million) provided the consumer demand exporting countries needed to keep their economies afloat. China's success hasn't been a short-term phenomenon. Over the past thirty years, government policies have helped the country create hundreds of millions of jobs, pulled half a billion people out of poverty, and taken steps to modernize and open up its carefully managed economic system.

Timmy Zhou, 29 years old, lives in Beijing and works as a product designer in a lottery company. When he was in high school, he thought the United States was better than China, because the Chinese government had a slogan that they would one day surpass the United States—a recognition of a gap between the two societies that weighed on Timmy's mind. When he went to college, classmates talked about moving abroad to the United States after graduation in search of a better future. Now their view of the United States has been tempered.

"My parents' generation has this impression that even

the moon seems fuller in the foreign lands than in China. They look at the U.S. at a distance and only see the good aspects of the society. People live in big houses and drive cars. The food they are eating is safer and the inflation is not that high," said Timmy. "After the financial crisis, my views are more objective. Life in the United States is not just about eating burgers and living in big houses."

Many young people are focusing on what life in China can offer instead. Most agree that the country is at a turning point and opportunities abound for its educated Generation Yers.

Ann He grew up in Zhuzhou, Hunan Province. She was the first person in her family to go to college, and studied information management at Jishou University. She went on to work for Foxconn, the world's largest manufacturer of electronic components, in Shenzhen. After four years, Ann was recruited by headhunters for a position in Beijing to work as a cost management specialist in an information technology company, and she moved up the economic ladder from manufacturing into high-tech. Her parents spent their lives in the countryside, and now, at 30 years old, Ann works in the capital city in a position for which her employers sought her out. She has no reason to be anything but optimistic about her future.

"Before I came to Beijing, the United States and Europe seemed to be very faraway places," said Ann. "Now my generation knows more about those places and we know they are not as good as my parents imagined."

"I think it's easier to be successful in China because it's such a huge country with so much demand. If you find the demand, it will be very easy to succeed."

Grace Fan, a 25-year-old journalist who travels between Shanghai, Guangzhou, and Beijing, says people's wealth is growing in general, and even more so for those launching their own businesses. She sees society as moving upward, in stark contrast to the views of most young Americans.

"I think China is becoming the new promised land," said Grace. "I feel that the scales are tilting towards the new markets."

However, this optimism is stymied by the restrictions on freedoms in China, which maintain the allure and promise of a different kind of opportunity in America. The personal stories shared by Chinese young people underscore how the American dream was never just about economic opportunity, but involved personal freedoms as well. The crisis has not changed that. For Generation Y in China, America still means something special, despite the growing possibility of greater economic success at home.

China is not completely a free-market economy, but a Communist Party–governed state that has been slowly introducing market-based economic reforms since the 1970s. Private businesses say they are always vulnerable to the attention of government officials, particularly if they are too successful. For instance, Wu Ying, once the sixth-richest woman in China, had built an empire that started with just a string of beauty parlors, but she was convicted of raising funds from "illegal sources," meaning lenders not owned by the government. Private borrowing is actually very common among nonstate businesses in China, where official bank loans usually go to state-owned enterprises, but this affair showed just how easy it is for the government to stamp out this forbidden market if it is tempted. In this case, many believe Wu Ying crossed a public official. Similarly, property ownership can be called into question by the government. In China, all property is considered to be owned by the state, and individuals can only possess land for a certain period of time, so it isn't guaranteed that one can pass on a piece of property to a child or spouse after death. With this rule, hundreds of thousands of people have been pushed off their land in the countryside to make way for urban development. These past actions underscore the power of government over individuals and are the very reason young Chinese still sometimes admire the United States, despite China's growing economic strength. While rules are changing and economic opportunities are growing, Generation Y still does not have the rights their counterparts in America often take for granted. Young people express distrust of the government, since the news and Internet are censored. It is well known that journalists are harassed and can face prison for reporting certain stories, while companies such as Google have to agree to restrictions on what Internet search results provide in order to access the Chinese market.

China's rise also hasn't been enough to counter what many young people say is an unfairness in society, where family background often plays a major role in access to well-paying jobs. They complain about the quality of education too, although there are signs of improvement: China's best universities, Tsinghua University and Peking University, recently joined the ranks of the top hundred in the world. Other issues members of Generation Y say are worse in China than in the rich West include poor air quality and food safety.

"The Chinese people still have this impression that people who have been abroad are much more capable than those who haven't been there," said Timmy. That's why he concludes, "If I had the opportunity, I would move to the United States. I don't think the *overall* situation in China is that good."

He's not alone, particularly among those who can afford to pack up all their things and head elsewhere. A survey of millionaires in China found that 60 percent were either considering moving abroad or already in the process of doing so—and most plans involved the United States.[13]

For Weiling Yu, this is out of reach. She is 24 years old and studies urban design at Guangzhou University. Weiling says a lot of her classmates dream about making a new life in the United States, but going overseas is too expensive for her—not just the move, but what she expects a good life to cost in the United States.

"I think their life quality is much higher than us. But I think it would be harder for people from the lower class like me to have a good life there. I'm getting more information about the United States and Europe as I grow. I heard stories about people going abroad but end up living a life not so fancy," said Weiling, referring to the difficulty of climbing up the economic ladder in the United States "My family is not that wealthy to be able to provide me such an amount of money."

The stories from China show that while the United States is facing some tough competition, it has not yet completely lost its luster. The United States is home to unique economic traditions and freedoms that help make the country the global force it is.

"It's a country where people are always looking for

solutions for their problems, and they have no prejudice against trying all different kind of ideas. That's really nice," said Eduardo from Brazil.

The United States must channel that spirit and make major reforms in order to secure a strong future for Generation Y, particularly given what the government has planned next.

6

Battle for Generation Y's Future: America's Deficit Versus Growth

PETER: People of Quahog, I have something to say. Now that we've freed ourselves from the terrible shackles of government, it's time to replace it with something better. The first thing we need is a system of rules that everyone must live by. Got to have rules. And since we can't spend all our time making rules, I think that we should elect some people to represent us, and they should make rules and choices on our behalf. That's probably a good idea. Now, this may be kind of expensive, so I got a plan: everyone should have to give some money from their salaries each year. Poor people will give a little bit of money and rich people will give a larger amount of money, and our representatives will use all that money to hire some people who will then provide us with social order and basic services. Now, it won't be perfect. Some of our representatives may end up being bastards. But you know what? That's okay because later we're going to have more elections, and we can use those elections to get rid of the bad guys and replace them with good guys, and then the system will just keep going on and on just like that. So who's with me? Will you join me in trying this new crazy thing?

—Family Guy, Season 10, Episode 1, "Tea Peter"

As the United States government crafts economic reforms to recover from this crisis, leaders now risk weighing down Generation Y even more. Political debates on the nation's deficit have confused priorities for the United States and its future. Rather than focus on the long-term joblessness, unstable work opportunities, and mounting student debt weighing on America's young, the government is on track to create a scenario that looks to replicate the mistakes of Europe by focusing on austerity, when the economy and Generation Y are in desperate need of support.

What Market Pressure? Politicians Make Bad Economists

The slow recovery after the recession has accelerated the rise of the nation's debt and deficit to their highest levels since World War II. The deficit, the difference between how much the government owes and how much it receives, quintupled between 2007 and 2010, when government coffers took a hit on both sides of the ledger—what was coming in and what was going out. Tax revenues declined during the crisis due to depressed spending by consumers and businesses. At the same time, government costs rose since more people needed unemployment payments and other public services. Spending also increased for emergency programs, including the $700 billion bailout for banks, insurers, and carmakers.

In general, over the long term, high deficits are bad because they are unsustainable. The government must take on additional debt, and more and more of the government's money goes toward paying interest on its debts. As a result, the government has less money to spend on growth-stimulating projects. At some point, the debt becomes so large that investors are expected to lose faith that the debtor government can pay them back—and a default occurs. In a more likely scenario, the value of the nation's currency ends up depreciating as the central bank is forced to print more money to pay for debts. Europe reached the point where investors lost faith and starting pulling out their money, which is why many countries implemented austerity measures to avoid a default.

But the United States is not Europe. The United States isn't even close to suffering Europe's fate. Its financial markets aren't yet under any immediate stress from the country's high deficit or debt. Part of the reason is that the United States is the most important and largest financial market in the world. Even after Standard & Poor's down-graded the credit rating of the nation's sovereign bonds in 2011, for the first time ever, the cost of government borrowing on credit markets was little affected. The yield on United States Treasuries, which is the rate the gov-ernment has to pay investors to borrow money on capi-tal markets, actually declined since the downgrade. This trend was helped in part by the crisis in Europe, which drove investors to seek safety in United States bonds, con-firming that in times of uncertainty America is still seen as the safest place for investors. In a world where most major economies are in trouble, the United States deficit is not in itself an impairment to government financing, because the United States is still the most reliable debtor and investors have few alternatives.

Despite this market reality, fear-mongering in the United States has led to a severe austerity program to ease the deficit. The driving force behind the "destructive push toward austerity" was ideological—a chance to move to-ward a reduction in the size of government—and not about economics, says Mark Thoma, an economics professor at the University of Oregon and author of the closely fol-lowed blog *Economist's View*.[1] Hatched in a bitter politi-cal compromise between Republicans and Democrats in

2011—each side aiming to *show* it has a stronger understanding of what's good for the economy, rather than *doing* what is actually good for the economy—the Budget Control Act of 2011 aims to dramatically cut back on government spending to counter the deficit. As approved, it would enact $1.2 trillion in automatic spending cuts, beginning in 2013 and extending over the next eight years. This will result in a more than 8 percent cut in domestic programs in the first year alone. Notably, these cuts wouldn't touch the programs that secure the United States' "middle-age consumption systems"—Medicaid and social security. The cuts carve out funding from the sciences and research, infrastructure, education, unemployment benefits, and low-income housing assistance, and would eliminate President George W. Bush's tax cuts, President Barack Obama's payroll tax cuts, and emergency unemployment benefits.[2]

This plan would amount to a severe blow to the United States economy if instituted as scheduled. In testimony to the Senate in March 2012, Federal Reserve chairman Ben Bernanke warned: "I think that we can achieve the very desirable long run fiscal consolidation . . . but we can do that in a way that doesn't provide such a severe shock to the economy in the near term."

But some lawmakers have argued that even deeper budget cuts are necessary now to domestic programs, such as AmeriCorps, a federal service program. Theresa Liszkay knows the risks all too well, and she is grateful AmeriCorps survived a previous round of cuts so she could take advantage. After graduating with a psychology degree from Wittenberg University in Ohio, the only job she could find in 2011, at age 23, was with AmeriCorps. The federally funded service program paid her a $10,000 annual stipend to volunteer for SON Ministries, a nonprofit organization in Hilliard, Ohio, that partners with local churches to support families in poverty. AmeriCorps also supports volunteers who help communities respond to natural disasters, teach young students computer skills and literacy, and work with other local groups like SON Ministries. For Theresa, it wasn't much money, but it was better than nothing.

"If the Obama administration had not reversed the Republican cuts to AmeriCorps, I would probably still be unemployed," said Theresa. "Service years have helped fill the unemployment gap for recent graduates. It is a great experience."

Demand for programs like AmeriCorps have increased during the crisis, since so many young people can't find work. Reducing their funding would not only threaten experiences like Theresa's and opportunities for Generation Y to get ahead, but also hurt the communities AmeriCorps operates in and supports. For instance, City Year, just one AmeriCorps program, is fighting the country's high school dropout crisis by tutoring and mentoring students who otherwise would have fallen through the cracks due to a lack of funding to pay regular teacher or guidance counselor salaries for the same type of support system. Since its inception in 1988, City Year has graduated more than fifteen thousand alumni.

And yet one plan for deeper spending cuts proposed by Paul Ryan as House Budget Committee chairman, named the Path to Prosperity, pushed for trillions in reductions, more than half of which would impact programs for the low-income and hurt those already suffering from the depressed economy, serving to further expand the inequality gap in America. While Medicare and Medicaid require serious reforms in the wake of the crisis, this is the austerity solution, which has left Generation Y hopeless and angry in Europe—even as Mr. Ryan warns that the United States shouldn't turn into Europe. Confusingly, he said while campaigning as the vice presidential candidate in 2012: "If we copy and follow European economics, we will copy and follow European results."[3]

Although the 2011 budget law may still be altered, and many expect lawmakers to keep delaying implementation, its very existence in the midst of crisis, when Generation Y's prospects are already at stake and economic growth is so fragile, shows Washington's carelessness with our future for the sake of a political victory—a frightening reality.

"I didn't expect to be in this situation," said Dean Baker, cofounder of the Center for Economic and Policy Research in Washington, D.C., in an interview. "I thought we had this horrible thing happen with this horrible collapse of the bubble . . . and now the government will spend money. The basic point is we need the government to support the economy at least for a period of time. I didn't really think that would be called into question."

He said there might be some reason to focus on the deficit if there was pent-up demand in the economy for housing, which could bring the economy back from the brink. But given that the impetus of the crisis was over-valued houses and the market they created, this isn't the case. Or, if the Federal Reserve's record low interest rates were doing enough to restore jobs and growth, but they're not. The United States central bank has slashed its federal funds rate to a range of 0 percent to 0.25 percent, yet people remain jobless and growth remains mired. Moreover, the Bank for International Settlements concluded in 2012 that as a result of "insufficient action" by the government to address the nation's economic problems, the positive effects of the Federal Reserve's extraordinarily low rates are shrinking, whereas the negative side effects may be growing.[4] "We need something to replace the demand that was being generated by the housing bubble. The only thing that can really do that is the government," said Baker.

So why has a long-term fiscal issue been thrust into the spotlight with calls for immediate and extensive action, given the negative effects already visible in Europe from this policy and the trust financial markets have in the United States? Political gain in a contentious and party-centric America. Politicians are in it to win it. Most aren't economists or academics with deep knowledge of these issues—or perhaps even any interest in them. Their interest is just in getting reelected and keeping their jobs, which means they will take an extreme position merely to hammer home a point, or pursue reforms that aren't necessarily good for the public at large but which may win favor with an important demographic or financial contributor. Financial contributions get politicians into office, and it is a small group of big donors that give the most. This has been explored by Thomas E. Mann and Norman J. Ornstein in *It's Even Worse Than It Looks: How the American Constitutional System Collided with the New Politics of Extremism*, Lawrence Lesig's *Republic, Lost: How Money Corrupts Congress—and a Plan to Stop It*, and Jack Abramoff's *Capitol Punishment: The Hard Truth About Washington Corruption from America's Most Notorious Lobbyist*.

In the 2012 presidential campaign season, new rules removed caps restricting the amount of money that corporations, unions, or individuals are allowed to contribute to political campaigns via the establishment of super political action committees, or super PACs. By definition, these super PACs can raise infinite amounts of money to promote or bash political candidates, although they cannot donate money directly to candidates. In practice, they allow a small group of billionaires to influence elections. A number of those donors are affiliated with the Tea Party, so it's not surprising that politicians have been pandering to this richly funded group, whose influence was reaffirmed when it helped raise resistance in 2011 to increasing the country's debt ceiling, a legal limit on the amount of money the United States government can borrow to pay its bills. Without an increase, the United States government would not have been able to meet its financial obligations. Certain lawmakers were effectively threatening not to pay back America's debts on time and send the country into default. Republicans used this as a political maneuver to show they are strict money managers, although they later agreed to raise the limit. At a moment when the economy was already vulnerable, this heated debate—not the deficit itself—actually posed the biggest financial market risk to the United States. In fact, Standard & Poor's said it was motivated to downgrade the country's credit rating by the drama that surrounded raising the debt ceiling: "The kind of debate we've seen over the debt ceiling has made us think the United States is no longer in the top echelon on its political settings," John Chambers, chairman of S&P's sovereign ratings committee, told the *Wall Street Journal*.[5]

This is a disappointing reality for Generation Y. It has little influence in Washington and yet the decisions made in the Capitol will burden this generation for decades. And as the Budget Act remains open for further debate, it is clear that any adjustment will again happen in a similar drama of partisan politics, further weighing on business and consumer confidence, as well as what's left of Generation Y's economic future.

To be clear, the United States' large debt and deficit are important problems that require consistent and gradual policy reforms. The government must commit to serious changes for the next decade in the way the United States spends and taxes for the sake of Generation Y and America's future. But it has more time to make these reforms, and it has always been the country's prerogative to take advantage of its privileged place in the world.

History Is Not on Austerity's Side

Historically, austerity in the United States during times of crisis has shown itself to be ineffective. During the Great Depression, slashed government budgets and higher interest rate policies by the central bank in the early 1930s, amid fears of a rising deficit, were responsible for the backslide in the economy and turned a terrible situation worse, as explored by Michael Lind in *Land of Promise: An Economic History of the United States* and in writings by Nobel Prize–winning economist Paul Krugman, including *End This Depression!* While central banks are keeping lending rates low this time around, the government doesn't look like it's learned its lesson. Spending cuts led to reduced tax revenues, and business and consumer activity declined. That meant less money went into the government or circulated inside the economy, annulling any of the expected benefits from saving federal money through spending cuts in the first place. One hundred leading economists pled the same logic that emerged from the Great Depression in a 2008 letter to the governor of New York during the crisis in an effort to fend off more state budget cuts:

> The reasoning is straightforward: in a recession, you want to raise (or not decrease) the level of total spending—by households, businesses and government—in the economy. That keeps people employed and buying things, and makes it more likely that businesses will want to invest to serve that consumer demand. Budget cuts reduce the level of total spending. Raising taxes on high income households also will reduce spending, but by much less than the amount of the tax increase since those with plenty of income typically spend only a fraction of their income. By contrast, almost every dollar of state and local government spending on transfer payments to the needy and for the salaries of public servants providing vital services to our communities enters the local economy right away, generating a greater economic impact.[6]

Economists Carmen Reinhart and Kenneth Rogoff, who literally wrote the book about the need for governments to take their debts more seriously, *This Time Is Different: Eight Centuries of Financial Folly*, and analyzed eight hundred years of national financial crises, now say that excessive cuts in the midst of the crisis isn't the answer. "I'm not saying you run out and pull the plug and have an adjustment that could derail what fragile recovery we do have," Reinhart told McClatchy Newspapers. Her colleague added that the United States may in fact need another stimulus bill, in contrast to politicians who have used their famous book to argue for immediate action on deficits.[7]

In other words, get the United States economy back on track first. It is common sense.

After all, the last stimulus bill in 2009 did work: the spending programs enacted immediately after the crisis stabilized the economy and offset potentially greater losses. The American Recovery and Reinvestment Act of 2009 provided tax cuts and increased federal funds for entitlement programs, such as unemployment benefits. The Congressional Budget Office calculated that these measures effectively boosted GDP and helped create jobs, and that the immediate effects on the deficit would automatically ease over a five-year horizon. The program prevented more than six million Americans from falling below the poverty line, according to the Center on Budget and Policy Priorities. Well into 2011, data showed that money from the Recovery Act was still helping to keep up to two million people in jobs.

Unfortunately, the effects of the 2009 program are waning. The Congressional Budget Office says the effects of the Recovery Act on economic output peaked in the first half of 2010 and have since diminished, while any support it offered for the job market began to wane at the end of 2010. As the aid funding dried up, the economy turned fragile again. Growth became weak and uneven in 2010 and into 2011. The facts are clear: the United States economy is recovering more slowly than expected because the government has been too scared to go further with stimulus spending or investing more in existing smart programs. The government is being held back by the deficit, and deficit hawks in Congress. However, by prioritizing economic growth and investing money in good programs to create jobs in the short term, the government could reap more tax money from a rise in salaries and consumer confidence in the longer term, and the economy can improve—and then the United States could take more decisive measures to resolve its deficit and debt.

Politicians Paralyzed by Fear in Midst of Crisis

Angel Gurria, secretary-general of the Organization for Economic Cooperation and Development, argues that there has been a systematic underestimation of the job creation and stimulus funding needed during the crisis in the United States, because the government was overly cautious of spending.

"This is something I think which was wrong. People did not do what was obvious in terms of the need. The need was the jobs," he said. "I can understand the logic. But frankly, it was an emergency."

Gurria, the former finance minister of Mexico, is worried that Congress and its political parties can't agree on a paced and selective reduction of the deficit, or embark on a fair analysis for potential reforms of entitlement programs such as social security. He is especially worried about the Budget Control Act's automatic cuts set to start in 2013.

"The [Budget Act] mechanisms are very blunt, are very large, [and] are very immediate. They do not have any intelligent moderation to accommodate the present situation. You are effectively going to see a too fast adjustment—and that will bring growth down too fast and too far, and you want to pace it a little bit," said Gurria. Unlike other smaller nations, he added, "the United

States can always issue a bond" to raise money. Its market is just that big and important.

"In the case of the United States, we have been suggesting that perhaps they should not be in such a rush to go for fiscal consolidation, that perhaps a paced, more gradual approach over a ten-year period is a proper way," he said. "Produce a situation where more jobs are created, less unemployment, less social costs, more demand . . . and also a greater sense of confidence in tomorrow—this is very important."

What's the Best Way to Address the Deficit into the Future?

While an adjustment in certain spending policies will be necessary to rebalance the economy, effective taxation has been shown to be a more successful tool in tackling gaps in governments' budgets than broad-stroke budget cuts, as argued in the 2008 letter by a hundred economists. Money spent by the government in federal programs is usually filtered back into the economy via spending, while well-constructed tax policy, especially taxes on higher income brackets, tends not to have as much impact on private spending, because well-off individuals save more of their income anyway. During the 1950s and early 1960s, when economic growth and the stock market were strong, tax rates were above 90 percent for the top tax bracket, compared to 35 percent now. Incidentally, economic growth and job creation were more robust after President Bill Clinton raised taxes than after President George W. Bush cut taxes.

Bush passed tax cuts on income and capital gains for high- and lower-income groups in 2001 and 2003, pushing the budget into deficit following four years of surplus. However, the reduction in taxes on capital gains—that's revenue that emerges from investments in stocks or real estate—is thought to have benefitted the wealthy in America in particular. Since then, GDP reached 3.6 percent in 2004 and from there went on a downward path—three years before the housing bubble even burst. If the cuts are allowed to expire, the Congressional Budget Office estimated, between 2012 and 2014 revenues into the government would increase by more than 30 percent.[8] Other policies during the Bush administration also propelled the deficit higher. The war in Iraq proved much more expensive than initially thought: spending on the defense budget doubled from 2000 to 2007.

Between the policies of the 1950s and the Bush era, there is room for government to meet in the middle to strengthen tax collection and improve the system for Generation Y's future. For instance, some corporations avoid paying any United States taxes at all by establishing offices in countries with more flexible tax regimes, such as Ireland or Luxembourg, which allow them to dodge payments or significantly reduce them. Moreover, many people in the top tax bracket take advantage of schemes that permit them to do the same, which in some cases means that someone in a middle-class tax bracket pays more taxes to the government than a wealthier person who theoretically should be paying a much higher rate. Hedge fund managers are one example. Their income is often taxed as a capital gain instead of ordinary income, which would make their tax rate 15 percent instead of 35 percent. In comparison, some 25-year-old Generation Yer slaving away at some entry-level job and making $40,000 a year before taxes would be paying a rate of 25 percent. This provides another example of how the difficulty for Generation Y to climb up the economic ladder is a systemic issue.

Famed investor and billionaire Warren Buffett, who says he is taxed at a rate of 17.4 percent, summed it up in an op-ed piece in the *New York Times*: "While the poor and middle class fight for us in Afghanistan, and while most Americans struggle to make ends meet, we mega-rich continue to get our extraordinary tax breaks . . . If you make money with money, as some of my super-rich friends do, your percentage may be a bit lower than mine. But if you earn money from a job, your percentage will surely exceed mine—most likely by a lot."[9]

The mega-rich don't pay payroll taxes like regular people, and they aren't even paying the rate set for someone making as much money as they do. These are loopholes, and government should work to fix them. That's just plain logical. Buffett suggests raising rates on taxable income, including dividends and capital gains, for those making more than $1 million, and raising rates even higher for those individuals who make $10 million or more, of which there were more than eight thousand in 2009. Another option is to reduce homeowner tax deductions, including for interest payments on mortgages—renters don't get to deduct their rent payments or any money they borrow to make those payments. Alternatively, the definition for the top tax bracket should be altered, as it is archaic in many ways. A small group of millionaires and billionaires who own most of the nation's wealth are taxed at the same rate as a two-income household that brings in $400,000 per year in regular jobs, positions that don't allow use of the same tax loopholes. When the president talks about raising the top tax rate, it can hit the latter household hard. While an income of, say, $250,000 isn't poor, it certainly doesn't mean living rich in America either. The introduction of more brackets to differentiate the rates for that top group is important to protect the middle class and their economic mobility. In addition, as a way of creating a bridge for those higher middle-income families to support a threatened Millennial generation, Americans could be allowed to make larger gifts to their children or other young people, perhaps directly into their social security or retirement accounts, without the recipient being taxed on that money.

It boils down to this: the United States' needs during the financial crisis are hostage to an ideological debate rather than an economic imperative. That means the biggest threat to the United States economy is actually the people in charge. There is no real point to pursuing aggressive deficit correction measures in the United States now, but there is a very real need to boost growth. Some economists, including Paul Krugman and Dean Baker, say the government could restore the number of jobs and businesses lost with another cash infusion and stimulus plan, which would encourage private businesses to unlock a sum about double that amount that has been just sitting on the sidelines, waiting for the economy and policy makers to show signs of stability. The International Monetary Fund has also called on the United States to take more measures to inject the economy with the confidence it needs, spurring businesses to hire and consumers to spend. This would provide the government with the economic growth and leeway necessary to make sound budget reforms at a modest pace. After all, the country's debt-to-GDP ratio, currently

101 percent, can be represented as a fraction, which has a numerator (spending) and a denominator (growth). That means the ratio can be improved by stimulating growth as much as by decreasing spending. At the same time, a long-term plan on the deficit would keep investor concerns at bay, because America is the key global financial market and its bonds will always be in demand, so long as the government starts planning for the future. Such an approach could lay the foundation for a more secure economic future for Generation Y in America, without throwing us under the bus today. It also makes more sense.

7

The Right Budget Choices: From Education to the Workplace

There is nothing wrong with America that cannot be cured by what is right with America.

—President William Jefferson Clinton, inaugural address, 1993

Rome has grown since its humble beginnings that it is now overwhelmed by its own greatness. . . . We can endure neither our vices nor the remedies for them.

—Titus Livius, *Ab Urbe Condita,* a history of Rome

There are several additional choices leaders can take to improve the outlook for Generation Y, focusing on education, the transition into the workplace, wages, and keeping talent at home. The United States' competitive edge, and a fair chance for its younger generations, depends on the construction of better policies in these fields.

Education Reforms 101

Politicians understood the importance of prioritizing higher education early on in American history, when funding for colleges helped to produce leaders and entrepreneurs who modernized the country and propelled its innovative spirit.

In the late 1800s, federal money was used to build institutions of higher education that taught engineering and agriculture, the type of skills the country needed to train its citizens in, helping to expand the nation's food industry for a growing population and creating the talent that pushed the country to become a leader in technology. Later the GI Bill rewarded World War II veterans for their service with a college education, cementing the importance of a degree to success in America. From the 1950s through the 1970s, federal funding supported the growth of research universities. The government also set up Pell Grants to help low-income families send their children to school.[1]

Today, Generation Y is practically required to have a university degree to get ahead. If America wants Generation Y and the country to get ahead, the federal government needs to make that degree more accessible again and ensure that it offers the graduate value in the real world. That means going beyond a hodgepodge of grants and scholarships, which only address a symptom rather than tackle the roots of the problem: out-of-control tuition, due to both poor funding and competitive pricing, as also argued by Ronald G. Ehrenberg, director of the Cornell Higher Education Research Institute, in *What's Happening to Public Higher Education? The Shifting Financial Burden.* Properly funding public universities again would help offset the catastrophic rise of college tuitions and provide more resources to increase the quality of education, so that these institutions produce graduates who can compete globally. For private universities, the government could create more incentives and stricter oversight. Some top-tier universities, such as Harvard and Princeton, have independently implemented measures to reduce costs for lower-income families, but not all private universities have followed suit.

Government has a role in American higher education, because education is central to citizens' way of life and future health. It is no different from the need to regulate food production or health care. As the United States faces growing risks to its dominance in the world, the nation must rely on an educated workforce to innovate its way out of an economic abyss. Now sure would be an irresponsible time for the American government to renege on its promise of an educated society.

Part of the solution in tackling college expenses may also lie in devising new ways for students and their families to pay for the cost of education. University of California students have offered a creative proposal, since state and federal budget cuts have made it all but impossible for the university to survive without raising tuition while also cutting resources and faculty, ultimately making students pay more for less. The student-led FixUC group penned the UC Student Investment Proposal, calling on the university to pay for all accepted students' education up front and allow graduates to repay the institution later, after securing employment. The school would consider each student an investment in the college's future—and the country's—and could expect high returns once the student scores a nice job with his or her degree. This makes the school accountable for delivering high-quality education and for connecting students with real-world opportunities. It would also diminish the burden on students and their families, shifting payment responsibilities away from parents who should be focusing on saving for retirement. In the University of California students' plan, after graduation alumni would repay the university with 5 percent of their income, interest-free, for the next twenty years of employment. They also propose incorporating, as an option, caps on minimum and maximum income thresholds for contribution. So, graduates would not begin making payments until their income exceeds $30,000 annually, and no earnings above $200,000 annually would be subject to the percentage contribution. The university wins with this program too, as it would actually bring in more money to the school than the way tuition is currently charged. A graduate who earns $50,000 annually (assuming that income doesn't increase over the course of twenty years, which one hopes it will) would pay back the university $50,000 over that time—several thousand dollars above current fees for an in-state student to attend the University of California. Meanwhile, graduates who choose higher-paying fields and earn double that, $100,000 annually would end up contributing $100,000 to the university. That is an investment that pays back more than 200 percent. It is important to note that this structure wouldn't punish those who choose lower-paying professions, such as social work or teaching, which are still vitally needed. This system would also encourage a greater alumni community—potentially strengthening fund-raising and job opportunity networks.

"[One] of the goals of the UC Student Investment Proposal is to encourage a shift in thought about the education students receive by attending the university, and their relationship with that university after graduation. Students will begin to think about the value of their education and its significance in the trajectory of their life from graduation to retirement," said the proposal text.

Private start-ups have launched since the crisis with the

same idea, including Upstart, which allows college students to raise money from private investors in exchange for a fraction of their future earnings. "By becoming an upstart, you are telling the world and your backers that you want to build a compelling and worthwhile career. And you're committed to repaying the backers who have taken a chance on you," says the company. In this way, small groups of private people are trying to work around the system to create a fairer marketplace. Still, their reach is limited and the system remains unchanged.

Another idea that has been debated to help students fund college education is through public service programs. Elizabeth Warren, a senator who also served as a special adviser on the Consumer Financial Protection Bureau and chairperson of the congressional oversight panel that oversaw the Troubled Asset Relief Program, proposed one such idea in 2007 with Sandy Baum, an independent policy analyst for the College Board and economics professor at Skidmore College, and Ganesh Sitaraman, an assistant professor at Vanderbilt Law School.[2] Their idea, titled Service Pays, would increase the amount students can borrow from the unsubsidized Stafford Loan Program to fund a full four years of college, including tuition, fees, and room and board, regardless of income. Currently it is a limited, low-interest federal loan program that subsidizes interest payments for qualifying students. (The 2011 Budget Control Act eliminates the subsidized interest rate payment option on Stafford Loans for graduate and professional students.) In the new program, the dollar amount of the available loans would be pegged to average prices at public four-year colleges and universities, and students would not be required to commit to public service as part of the terms of their loan. However, the government would forgive students one year of college expenses for each year they work in public service after college. If they work for four years, their college loans would be completely paid off. Whatever loans students don't work off can be repaid through regular repayments. Besides military careers, Service Pays participants could work in a revamped Peace Corps that would place young people with aid and development organizations around the world, for the federal or state government, or for other civil agencies.

The Brookings Institution said the creation of such a program would build a recruiting and training ground for future diplomats and aid officials, as well as treasury and homeland security experts. In a survey the research institute conducted of more than a thousand young Americans, when Brookings asked if, like the military academies, they would be interested in committing to serve government for five years after graduation in exchange for free education, 71 percent responded positively.[3] Some versions of such a program already exist today, but they are not as supportive or sweeping. For instance, the College Cost Reduction and Access Act allows students to work off their student loans in public service careers, but only after the graduate makes monthly loan payments and works for government, both for ten years. Well-endowed private institutions have gone further. Yale Law School's Career Options Assistance Program, a model for other law schools, encourages graduates to take on lower-paying jobs in nonprofit organizations or in the public interest by forgiving their debts.

Whichever path is taken, the government should think seriously about devising a way for young people to obtain a higher education so that they can *effectively* contribute to the future of this country in the public or private sectors—without overwhelming debts.

For those already spending on education, the way students pay back college loans requires a closer look. So far, recent attempts at introducing more leeway only benefit new students. For instance, after the crisis, President Obama lowered the repayment cap on federal education loans to 10 percent of the debtor's discretionary income and moved the loan forgiveness deadline to twenty years from twenty-five years for eligible students. William E. Brewer Jr., president of the National Association of Consumer Bankruptcy Attorneys, advises a much broader plan, particularly as private sector loans have become the most problematic for borrowers. Their high interest payments and larger loan sizes contribute to some of the toughest debt situations for Millennials, says Brewer. That's why Congress should roll back laws to how they used to be, when there was a statute of limitations on the length of time a creditor has to sue a borrower who defaults on college debts. That way, college debts could be forgiven. In 1991, new laws eliminated any statute of limitations on student loans, so a graduate could be in default for fifteen years and suddenly get sued by a loan company. Before that, in the 1970s, laws were put in place so that students couldn't rid of the debt through bankruptcy. Both of these laws have proven disastrous for students, affecting their lives indefinitely. Unpaid student loans stay on the borrower's credit record even seven years after the debtor pays off the loan, making it harder for him or her to take out any other loans, buy a house, or even get a job.

However, reforming the student loan industry is a tough endeavor, because the banking industry spends millions of dollars to lobby against reformation. The *Chronicle of Higher Education* reported that in recent years the leading participants in the government's bank-based loan program spent almost $14 million lobbying the government, even as the recession gripped the country and banks struggled from the effects of the credit crunch, to try to save their role in the student debt machine.[4] There are also hurdles from the universities, which historically have had a close relationship with lenders. In 2007, an investigation by the New York attorney general discovered that dozens of schools had received payments for steering students to specific lenders. Some school administrators even received stock in the lenders in exchange for placing these institutions on the school's list of preferred lenders.

Reforms are also needed to help families save and plan for college education costs. Going forward, saving is especially important, since it has become increasingly hard for some to tap loans after the crisis. Banks are no longer as open to one of the most popular financing options previously available, home equity loans, which offered lower rates than federal or private college loans and were tax deductible. The major savings option is the 529 college savings plan, created by Congress in 2001, which offers two alternatives. The first allows families to put savings into an investment vehicle, usually a mutual fund that is tax exempt or tax deductible. The money can be used to pay for study in any accredited college, but not for student loans or interest payments. However, this option is not reliable: it is still an investment in financial markets. In this way, the government is encouraging potentially risky investments that could see families' education savings actually decline in value. Indeed, during the crisis, some high school students saw funds earmarked for college reduced significantly. Instead, each state's 529 program could have at least one high-interest savings account that does not require a financial market investment but pays a higher interest rate than a normal savings account and is insured by the Federal Deposit Insurance Corporation (FDIC), so that families can enjoy the tax benefits without having to accept the market risk. (Saving is an even longer-term issue for Generation Y because stretched government finances make it unlikely that Millennials will be able to retire on social security. There needs to be education on this today, because saving takes time. In the same way the United States needs a 529 alternative, safe investment vehicles and savings programs for the younger generation's retirement would be an important and realistic policy step by the government, offering an alternative to the 401(k) program, which is exposed to market volatility and the whims of money managers.)

The second 529 option allows parents to plan for college in advance by buying credits at participating universities at current prices, before their children are ready to go and tuition costs rise. But the number of state schools participating in this option has declined by nearly half since the crisis, even as the private sector has maintained this as an option. The Tuition Plan Consortium, LLC, established a program that also allows families to prepay for credits at 270 participating institutions, including Massachusetts Institute of Technology, Vassar College, Rice University, and Stanford University, among others. However, since this route is primarily for private universities, costs are still obviously higher than many can afford, and those who hoped for a savings option for state schools cannot take advantage of the program.

So we're back to the fact that tuitions are too high for many students. If the education market expanded, though, to offer different kinds of paths to an accredited education respected by employers, there could be more price competition to create lower-cost options. Technology is the solution. Companies such as the Floating University, launched in 2011, aim to democratize higher education and have received a lot of positive attention—and even the time of top professors from the country's leading private universities. The Floating University distributes online multimedia curricula via video and text, featuring lectures by leading thinkers in various fields, from biology to the arts. It is a subscription service that charges less than $500 to participate in courses or seminars. The company's view of the industry: "The concept of a modern university as the nexus of research and teaching is no longer relevant in a world of Google and Yahoo! where all of the world's information is available at the click of a mouse. A new era has been ushered in. As the best teachers are now producing coursework that they can license independently of the institutions where they reside, our idea was to bring these courses to everyone, everywhere, anytime." But the Floating University doesn't give degrees, and degrees are the currency in America's labor market.

Meanwhile, for-profit institutions that do award degrees, an alternative to pricier universities or public colleges, have a bad reputation. There are a slew of online for-profit colleges, such as the University of Phoenix, that have gained in popularity in recent years through aggressive advertising and recruitment campaigns, often targeted at lower-income groups. The schools take advantage of Internet-based lessons, which make it easier for students to hold a job while studying. However, students at these for-profit schools are much more likely to take out loans than students at public colleges, and therefore graduate with a much higher level of debt. Moreover, they are twice as likely to default on their debt as public college students, according to the Department of Education, which suggests that for-profit college students are unable to secure the same type of work after graduation. That's led to charges by some that these schools are little more than marketing schemes, especially after an undercover investigation of fifteen such colleges by the General Accountability Office. All fifteen schools "made deceptive or otherwise questionable statements" to the GAO's undercover applicants, including exaggerating potential earnings after graduation and encouraging falsification of financial aid forms.[5] However, since budget cuts have struck community colleges, they are unable to meet demands for degree programs in fields such as nursing and engineering, for example, opening the way for these for-profit schools to attract more students.[6] With proper legislation and incentives, these institutions could become a more reliable alternative. However, recent efforts at reform focus on ensuring that graduates of for-profit colleges repay their loans, or else the for-profit schools risk losing out on federal student aid, which is their largest source of revenues. These efforts do not actually address the quality of education. This is not surprising, given the complex accreditation system for colleges in the United States. It is disconnected, with several bodies having authority over different regions, and then specialized national agencies, each with different standards. But if there were higher standards in place for private Internet-based schools and a more unified and thorough accreditation process, Generation Y would be provided with more options for securing a degree from an institution that offers students a competitive price and the flexibility to work while studying.

More-established public and private universities could also take advantage of Internet-based education to provide lower-cost options for students. Some, including the Massachusetts Institute of Technology, have already made strides in this direction by offering certain courses online. But so far, most of these initiatives give participants a certificate of completion at the end, rather than university credit toward a degree.

The issues of education costs and quality appear much earlier in a student's life too, even at the primary and secondary school levels. In the United States, the phrase "land of opportunity" means something only for families who can afford an expensive house in a good public school district. These school systems, mostly located in the suburbs, are like private schools, with a high quality of education, while people on the bottom two-thirds of the income ladder are stuck in public schools that are not doing as well. That's because most local schools are funded with property taxes, which in the United States are typically collected by local governments. The federal government contributes just about 10 cents to every dollar that is spent by local authorities on education from kindergarten through twelfth grade—an amount less than that found in the majority of countries in the world.[7] As a result, family income has become an increasing determinant in test scores: since 1976, differences in school test scores correlated with income has expanded up to 40 percent.[8] This divide in education is costing the United States economy a lot of money: all that potential talent and productivity are lost in an unfair school system. In fact, according to the OECD, if that loss were quantified, it would add up to more than the loss in output from the Great Recession. In effect, closing the education gap would recover the United States' economy, period.

In the OECD's latest Program for International Student Assessment, a global study of school systems, American public schools in which at least half of the students were eligible for free or reduced-price lunch scored below the overall OECD and United States averages in reading literacy. Schools in which less than 25 percent of students were eligible scored above the average. The cause traces back to money. In about half of all OECD member countries, disadvantaged schools tend to have more teachers per student. The United States is one of four countries—with Israel, Slovenia, and Turkey—that gives already advantaged students access to more teachers per student. That's why 17 percent of the variation in student performance across the United States is explained by students' socioeconomic background, compared to just 9 percent in Canada or Japan. And the OECD makes clear that the United States is not suffering with a greater number of socioeconomically disadvantaged students than other countries; rather, the way the system is constructed keeps them down, limiting economic mobility and a chance at equal opportunities. Education experts point to other countries, including Finland, where there is more equality in the education system, and how the United States can learn from their example. If the United States matched Finland's performance, which has one of the smallest gaps in the world between the weakest- and strongest-performing students, it could result in gains of $103 trillion for the economy.[9]

Finland's most notable tools for improving its education

system over the years have been the way the country trusts its teachers and the unification of all its schools. Finland empowered teachers and set national training standards for all educators. This has prepared teachers to become independent and exercise judgment over their classroom needs—and school administrators and the government trust their judgment. Teachers teach not to a test but to their specific classroom of students—a sign of confidence in educators' ability to judge their pupils' needs. As a result, schools respond quicker to students who are falling behind, with teachers taking on the responsibility of working one-on-one with students. Teachers are held in high esteem in Finland, making teaching an attractive career choice. Work conditions are better too. Schools and class sizes are smaller in Finland, and most schools try to keep teachers with the same group of students for several years. Each school also shares common national education goals, so all students have an equal chance at the same education wherever they go to school and whichever neighborhood they live in. Moreover, Finns do all this while spending less money per student than the United States already does.[10]

The path to reforming education and its funding must begin with government prioritizing these issues in the federal budget. One way to do this is to separate education and investment-for-the-future costs from the rest of the federal budget. One vocal advocate of this approach, particularly through the crisis, has been Robert B. Reich, who served as secretary of labor under President Clinton and on President Obama's transition economic advisory board. "It's a little nutty to treat public spending that keeps us comfortable today the same as public investment that expands our capacity to be productive in the future," said Reich, now a professor at the University of California at Berkeley. Reich supports a bold proposal that was debated back during the Clinton administration but which government hasn't pursued: split the total United States budget into two separate parts, creating one budget for capital expenditures, the type of spending that's more accurately described as an investment for the future, and one for operating costs. Reich argues that, like any business, the United States should be making capital investments up to the point where the return no longer justifies the expenditure. This separate budget would include education, infrastructure, and basic research and development—all areas that have been cut down by the crisis, and even years before that. Now that interest rates in the United States are at record lows, government could take advantage of the cheap funding and borrow money to spur investment today for a better tomorrow. "It's irrational not to borrow money to make investments where the return is substantially higher," said Reich. He's not the only one to say so. Alan Blinder, for instance, who served as vice chairman of the Board of Governors of the Federal Reserve System, wrote in the summer of 2012: "The U.S. government can now borrow for five years at about 0.75 percent and for ten years at about 1.7 percent. Both rates are far below expected inflation, making real interest rates sharply negative. Yet legions of skilled construction workers remain unemployed while we drive our cars over pothole-laden roads and creaky bridges. Does this make sense?"[11] The alternative is allowing the large income gap between the ultra-rich and everyone else in America to continue to grow, which, as discussed earlier, increases unwanted ills in society and ultimately threatens the economy. The fallout—and it's already happening—is that a large portion of the United States workforce will not be nearly as productive as it could be and will be consigned to low-wage jobs. As Reich said: "We are eating our seed corn."

A capital budget has been a long-running debate. Many aren't convinced that government spending for the future could be done responsibly.

Back in 1949, the Commission on Organization of the Executive Branch of the Government, chaired by former president Herbert Hoover, recommended that consumption and capital expenditures be separated in the federal budget. In 1967, another commission was formed, and this time it rejected a capital budget. President Ronald Reagan was an advocate for a capital budget in the 1980s, but the idea never went forward. In February 1999, a commission under President Bill Clinton advised against the creation of a separate capital budget, even though it concluded that "the current budget process does not permit decision-makers in the executive branch and Congress to pay sufficient attention to the long-run consequences of their decisions. This results in inefficient allocation among capital expenditures and shortchanges the maintenance of existing assets." Its report also made clear that members of the Clinton commission were by no means in consensus: "While the members of the commission endorse the recommendations presented herein, individual members do not necessarily agree with all of the analysis or with each and every word of the report."[12] Analysis by the Brookings Institution shows that the consistent problem over the decades has been that there just isn't enough political support for an independent capital budget. Moreover, debaters couldn't decide on a single definition of capital or determine whether the current budget format creates a deficit or a surplus in federal investment.[13] The Congressional Budget Office in a 2008 report highlighted the same complexities in establishing such a budget.[14] In the end, they concluded that this budget wouldn't actually improve federal *decision making* on infrastructure financing and comes with too many accounting problems. As Alec Ian Gershberg of the Milano Graduate School of Management and Urban Policy at the New School and Joseph F. Benning of the Robert F. Wagner Graduate School of Public Service at New York University wrote following the Clinton commission report: "If history is any guide, this can easily lead to much wasteful, pork-barrel spending all under the guise of 'investment.' "[15]

One alternative to a capital budget proposed by Representatives Rosa L. DeLauro, Keith Ellison, Anthony Weiner, and Steve Israel in 2009 and 2011, and supported by Brookings, is a national infrastructure bank, similar to the European Investment Bank that was established in 1958. While more modest than an entire capital budget, the bank would have a specific focus and thus could at least improve the federal investment and evaluation process for infrastructure projects (although this would exclude education).

Creating a Better Workplace and Worker

There is a lot that can be done to help graduates transition from school to the labor market. There is weak career counseling in schools and poor to nonexistent connections between the school and work systems. When students graduate, they are pushed into the world and told, "Good luck!" There is a positive side to this because it means there is a lot of flexibility in the United States labor market. There are multiple ways for someone to get a job. However, during a period of economic volatility, such as now, this flexibility exposes vulnerabilities in the system. Schools don't prepare graduates with specific job-based training, which is prolonging the amount of time young people spend as temporary or part-time workers—the kind of workers who are laid off during periods of economic uncertainty. Compounding the problem, employers don't typically invest in developing or training part-time workers, so they can remain unqualified for the workplace for years.

In contrast, Germany boasts intensive school-to-work programs, including apprenticeships, which result in low youth unemployment and a relatively easier transition for young people into the real world. Germany's youth unemployment rate is under 8 percent. The country has a multitrack education system that splits up children at a young age, usually fourth grade, onto different paths—one that gears children toward entering a university and others that set them on the course for vocational training in a specific field. Employers invest in the development of young workers, participate directly in their training, and usually hire the apprentices. And students who enter vocational training aren't consigned to only mechanical jobs. Unlike the United States, in Germany many jobs require only this type of career training, including professions such as nursing. (In the United States, nurses now graduate with an average student debt of more than $23,000, up from under $19,000 in 2004, according to the American Society of Registered Nurses.) While Germany's model narrows choices for children early in life, it produces workers that are better suited to the country's economic needs, and the results are robust and steady economic growth and reliable employment, without all the debt. The United States could use that type of thinking, especially as it directs so many young people into arrears to pay for college.

A report by the Harvard Graduate School of Education says that America's "college for all" mentality may be harming students—and not only by putting them into debt.[16] Only one-third of all jobs in the next decade will require a bachelor's degree from a four-year institution or a higher degree. Especially after the financial crisis, the report warns that "teens now face Depression-era employment prospects." The Georgetown Center on Education and the Workforce also forecasts that in the second decade of the twenty-first century, most job openings will not require a bachelor's or advanced degree. That's why the influential Harvard report argues that *any* post-high-school credential—including an associate's degree or an occupational certificate—should become the new American goal, particularly as only 56 percent of those enrolling in a four-year college have actually attained a bachelor's degree after six years, and less than 30 percent of those who enroll in community college succeed in obtaining an associate's degree within three years.

"We are the only developed nation that depends so exclusively on its higher education system as the sole institutional vehicle to help young people transition from secondary school to careers, and from adolescence to adulthood," said Robert Schwartz, academic dean and professor at the Harvard Graduate School of Education.[17] Most advanced nations place far more emphasis on vocational education, which doesn't suffer from as much of a stigma as in the United States. After the ninth or tenth grade in Austria, Denmark, Finland, Germany, the Netherlands, Norway, and Switzerland, between 40 percent and 70 percent of young people opt for a public education program that typically combines classroom and workplace learning over the next three years. The certificate at the end becomes "real currency in the labor market," says the report. And then, if these students want, they can still go to university afterward, with the benefit of practical experience. The Harvard analysis says America must broaden its range of high-quality options for young adults through more career counseling and career-focused education, as well as apprenticeship programs and community colleges that offer a practical pathway to well-paying jobs.

Employers have a role to play too. Like in Germany, employers should work with schools to offer job-based learning from an early age, so that there are actual jobs related to students' programs of study as they approach graduation and students have the exact skills employers want. For instance, the Harvard study suggests that in middle school, students would be exposed to career counseling and job shadowing. In high school, paid internships would offer the chance at deeper exposure to a certain field. At the post-secondary level, employers should take a more active role in collaborating with colleges to communicate exactly what knowledge and skills they want to see in employees. At the higher education level, employers would be able to teach some of those requirements through part-time jobs, which are an essential element missing from the education system, as most college students must work in jobs completely unrelated to their programs of study. The United States government could build incentives for the private sector to take on this role.

At the very least, the United States government should do more to educate young people about their options. It could also consider working toward changing the credentials for certain careers, such as nursing, which only recently started to require a four-year university degree, so that one doesn't have to go into debt to obtain a job. It could also focus training in the final years of high school, for those who are interested, on different high-skilled technical careers in engineering, technology manufacturing, or hospital patient care; these programs could transition to specialized training in a community college setting, offering a rewarding alternative to a four-year liberal arts degree. This is particularly important for young men, because they are more likely to drop out of high school and less likely than women to receive a higher degree; an alternative path that leads to some technical certificate could go a long way in securing a more stable future for them. Economists say that men will become more vulnerable in the workplace because fields dominated by men who are dropouts or have lower degrees are shrinking.

Meanwhile, to encourage the hiring of young and new workers by businesses today, President Barack Obama had proposed tax credits for the companies who hire them, an idea supported by academics including Professor Harry Holzer of Georgetown University, formerly chief economist for the United States Department of Labor. But Obama's proposal stalled amid political fighting. Holzer has called for tax cuts for new hires and more robust tax credits for hiring and on-the-job training of young people.[18] Warning that low earnings will scar millions of young workers for years to come, even when the labor market fully recovers, Holzer added in testimony before the Senate Budget Committee in September 2011 that "employers that take the 'high road' in their human resources policies and provide career ladders and promotion opportunities for entry-level employees" should be offered tax credits too. Some states have taken it upon themselves to pursue incentives to hiring young people. For instance, New York passed its Youth Works Program, proposed by Governor Andrew Cuomo in 2011, which granted tax credits in 2012 to employers that hired and trained young inner-city workers, and kept them on the payroll.

Hurdles to a Self-Made Generation Y

Burned in the labor market, many Millennials are deciding to become entrepreneurs, but success isn't always at the end of their journey. It has become tougher and tougher to stay in business—any business—since the Great Recession began, which means that entrepreneurship, considered to be the backbone of the American economy and one of the only viable paths left for Generation Y, is becoming an even riskier proposition. From 2007 to 2010, small-business failure rates increased by 40 percent. Job creation rates from business start-ups were lower in 2009 than in any year since at least 1980.[19] This poses a problem not only for Generation Y but also for the American economy, which has always relied on entrepreneurs' ingenuity to create jobs. These companies have been one of the few engines of economic growth and employment in recent years, despite increasing failure rates. Monthly national employment reports show that while government jobs are shrinking faster and faster, private sector payrolls are inching up with the help of fast-growing start-ups, particularly those utilizing new technologies. Recognizing the uniquely difficult economic landscape entrepreneurs now face, the government has launched initiatives, such as Startup America, which has partnered with private companies that have committed to investing more than $1 billion in services for start-ups. That includes loaning computers and contributing free tax services. Startup America is just at its beginning, but groups such as the Young Entrepreneur Council say this still doesn't go far enough in encouraging young people to create their own jobs and showing them how to get started. The Youth Entrepreneur Council has been lobbying along with Young Invincibles, which aims to represent the interests of 18-to-34-year-olds in identifying solutions to America's opportunity challenges, for the Youth Entrepreneurship Act, legislation designed to open up opportunities for young people who want to start a business. The act includes student loan forgiveness programs, expanded access to microloans, and increased investment in entrepreneurship education programs. The point is to stop just talking to 18-year-olds about how Facebook was founded in some Harvard dorm room. Instead, actively reduce barriers for young people to secure business loans and increase mentoring and education programs.

Creating a More Competitive America for a Competitive Generation Y

Increasing entrepreneurship is about creating a more competitive economy for Generation Y's future. But a competitive economy also depends on ensuring that the people who give the United States its competitive edge have the chance to keep contributing.

Reforming visa rules to allow a greater number of educated foreigners to earn permanent residence would be a big step in strengthening the economy. H-1B visas, which allow United States employers to hire foreign workers for specific fields, are doled out to a limited number of recipients each year and for a limited period. The visas are tied to a specific employer, and the immigrant's ability to remain in the United States depends on continued employment with that sponsor, unless another company agrees to sponsor the person's visa. Always, the immigrant's presence in the country depends on an employer who can afford all the paperwork. This system allows foreign students who are already integrated into American society to slip away if they can't find employee sponsorship immediately, and disallows potential job creators from launching their own companies in the United States. In contrast, the United Kingdom grants permanent status to immigrants after five years. In Australia, many immigrants receive permanent visas from the outset. Australia has also focused on recruiting international students, who are often graduates of American universities, since these schools are the top in the world, even though America doesn't do much to keep that investment in the country. The Canadian Experience Class visa allows high-skilled workers with education or work experience to ask for permanent residence after two years in the country. The United States is losing out—a policy choice that is confusing given that these immigrants can fill important gaps in the economy, including the shortage of engineers. "Maintaining some kind of flow—hopefully better managed and better suited to our economic needs—should be the policy goal," said Audrey Singer, an immigration expert at the Brookings Institution.

If America's inflexibility on visa issues persists, it risks losing jobs that could be created for American-born Millennials. For example, in 2007 Microsoft expanded into Canada, rather than create more jobs in the United States, explicitly to recruit high-skilled professionals affected by immigration issues in the United States.[20] In another example, firms such as Google, eBay, and Yahoo! were all founded by immigrants, which in turn created many, many jobs, not just at those companies but at businesses based on their existence.

Gender equality is another key element of competitive and robust economies that the United States is behind on. While women in America hold more of the nation's higher-degree diplomas than men, they are still not given an equal chance at the executive table, in large part due to inhibiting policies. On the Economist Intelligence Unit's Women's Economic Opportunity Index, an assessment of laws and attitudes that affect women workers and entrepreneurs, the United States ranks below most of the leading industrialized economies: Canada, Sweden, Belgium, Norway, Finland, German, Iceland, the Netherlands, France, Portugal, Denmark, the United Kingdom, New Zealand, and Australia. This is in direct contrast to today's economic needs. Families increasingly rely on women's salaries, particularly amid economic volatility, but women still earn just 77 cents for every dollar paid to their male counterparts in the same job. This gap in earnings translates into $10,784 less per year in median earnings, leaving women and their families shortchanged.[21] It's not such a surprise given that the United States ranks seventy-eighth in the world for female legislative representation, sandwiched between Venezuela and Turkmenistan, and fewer than twenty companies in the Fortune 500 are run by women. But it is a disappointment, especially since the International Monetary Fund, among many other institutions, says that reducing gender inequality and improving the status of women may contribute to higher rates of economic growth and greater macroeconomic stability.[22] As Secretary of State Hillary Clinton put it in a speech at the Asia Pacific Economic Cooperation's Women and the Economy Summit in September 2011: "[To] achieve the economic expansion we all seek, we need to unlock a vital source of growth that can power our economies in the decades to come. And that vital source of growth is women . . . Because when everyone has a chance to participate in the economic life of a nation, we can all be richer."

New policies could help pave the way to unleash the power of women in the workplace to support Generation Y and its future families. Economists at Bank of America Merrill Lynch say women's higher levels of education relative to men make them "well positioned for the jobs of the 21st century": women earned roughly 61 percent of the associate's degrees in the last ten years, 56 percent of bachelor's degrees, and 58 percent of master's degrees. In order for women to take advantage of these jobs, though, policies need to take into account the unique role of women. For instance, the United States is the only country on the *Economist*'s index that does not have legislation mandating maternity leave benefits. (In comparison, in Sweden, laws penalize men financially if they don't take paternity leave, in order to promote a more equal society. Since the government began encouraging men to take leave, female incomes have risen, as the maternity leave income penalty is slowly nullified.) And yet women are still expected to take care of children and family, and increasingly work too. That's why establishing job-protected family and medical leave for more workers would be an important step to shield Millennials from becoming unemployed because they need to care for a child.

"[Families] have needed Mom's earnings for quite some time. We didn't want to admit it because in doing so, we'd have to finally address how we were going to deal with all the things she used to do for us—for free—before she had a day job. And we'd need to make sure that she was paid fairly on the job," said Heather Boushey, senior economist for the Center for American Progress Action Fund, in testimony before the House Subcommittee on Workplace Protections in March 2009.

Building a more competitive America for Generation Y and the nation's future might also require better tools for measuring competitiveness. The Progressive Policy Institute (PPI) has proposed a Competitiveness Audit. It argues that an accurate industry-by-industry measure of global competitiveness would be an important tool in figuring out which American businesses can create jobs and how. PPI suggests that the Bureau of Labor Statistics evaluate and rank industries as globally competitive, uncompetitive, or near-competitive, depending on domestic prices compared to import prices. For example, the Bureau of Labor Statistics currently makes no calculations on whether a table from China costs less in the United States than a similar table made in North Carolina, and by how much. However, knowing the size of the price gap in furniture would make an enormous difference to a state such as North Carolina, which has lost 60 percent of its furniture-making jobs since 2001, many to China.

"If the price differential is only 10 percent, then some of those furniture-making jobs might come back as exchange rates adjust or as wages rise overseas. But if the price differential is 40 percent, those jobs are probably gone for good, and would unlikely be helped even by strategic investment," explains PPI.

As this exercise is repeated over time, PPI suggests it will become possible to tell whether price gaps are widening or closing, with the audit serving as a benchmark for businesses to act on. The audit could also guide government spending to areas that are most competitive, so that public funds are no longer committed to failing industries. "Using available resources to promote job growth in a targeted, effective way is crucial—and that requires better data," PPI says in its proposal.[23]

But even if government purses some of these policies, it is clear that some of the consequences from the financial crisis are probably unavoidable at this point for Generation Y, following years of unfavorable decisions and the way the crisis has dragged on. Moreover, relying on leaders to take these measures is probably a naive strategy for America's young. There are just some realities Millennials will have to face. Generation Y will have to find ways to save itself, to create its own version of The Good Life.

8

How Generation Y Can Save Itself

ANGELA: This life has been a test. If this had been an actual life, you would have received instructions on where to go and what to do.

—*My So-Called Life*, Season 1, Episode 7

While the crisis may be threatening America's future in all of the ways described in this book, America's future is attempting to reinvent itself.

Generation Y is already adapting to this new American life, finding ways to thrive and succeed even as the economy remains in the dumps. They are changing careers and moving to new cities. Some are writing their own playbook and are becoming entrepreneurs. Generation Y is facing this crisis head-on, with many already living by the advice of Reid Hoffman, cofounder of LinkedIn, who has encouraged people to think of their careers as in a permanent state of beta. *Beta* is the term regularly used for the initial testing period of new technologies. It is a period of continuous growth and improvement, and a concept Generation Y must become very comfortable with.

Generation Y is primed to find meaningful work that makes a difference, a goal they rank above even money, according to a survey by MTV. Generation Y wants to connect deeply with their work. Half of those polled would "rather have no job than a job they hate," and 95 percent are "motivated to work harder when I know where my work is going." They are guided not by a sense of self-importance but by a desire to contribute and be heard. These are the types of response one would expect from a generation raised to believe in the American dream and that education and hard work will result in achieving one's goals.[1]

What Millennials Want/Can Have From Work

CREATIVITY

Jennifer Gargotto is about to celebrate her 25th birthday. But instead of thinking about a birthday party or gifts, she is mainly thinking about work, after launching her own business six months ago.

Jennifer grew up in Denver, Colorado, and spent two years in journalism school at New York University before switching to the University of Colorado, Boulder, where she earned a degree in psychology in 2010. After struggling to find full-time work—even applying to work as a house cleaner—Jennifer landed a "prestigious" marketing position in a Denver-based technology company that helps organize conferences and trade shows. The post paid $30,000 annually, offered no benefits, and required her to work more than fifty hours per week. After a year, despite the difficulty in finding the job in the first place, she decided to quit. Jennifer reasoned that she could take the skills she had developed and create a business of her own that would be more lucrative and more fulfilling than her desk job.

Jennifer started her own women's blog network, posting

news on health and relationships, as well as lifestyle features. She linked up with other bloggers like her around Denver, enlisted the help of friends and family, and managed to grow the traffic to her website dramatically. Now she is devising ways to monetize the blogs by selling some of her content and building alliances with retailers to market products through her website.

Jennifer credits her previous job—and the harsh economic climate—for her success. "If I had just gone out and got a great job, I would have never had the courage to start this on my own," she said. "I would have never done this had it not been for the crisis."

In this new economy, Generation Y can't rely on old business ways. It has to innovate. It has to use its college education in creative ways: to discover new business models, new technologies, and new consumer demands. That means reinventing the way some local corner shop does business just as much as developing a new social network. Generation Y has no choice but to create new things to get ahead.

Consider Angela Betancourt, 29. Bogged down by student loans and a low-paying job in public relations—an industry very much affected by corporate budget cuts due to the financial crisis—Angela was frustrated that at almost 30 years of age she still couldn't afford to buy an apartment in Miami. She even does extra freelance work on the side to supplement her income, just to get by. Hoping to earn more and take control of her future, Angela decided to launch an online clothing retailer, but a shopping portal that is unlike any other to date. The company aims to incorporate new technologies that would make the shopping experience "more fun," said Angela. She is in the early stages, but Angela says the company is her way of not becoming a "victim" of the financial crisis. Angela demonstrates the importance of tapping into Generation Y's edge: its comfort with technology. A study by the McKinsey Global Institute found that corporate leaders will need to sharpen their focus on the opportunities the Internet offers for new products and expanded customer reach, or else Internet technologies that can radically change markets will disrupt their business models.[2] Generation Y grew up understanding this. It is the first generation to be born with a computer in the house, and Millennials are usually the earliest adopters of new personal devices and technologies. Only by immersing itself in cutting-edge technology and new online-focused business models can Generation Y take advantage of that edge.

"The upside to the economic crisis is that it forces me to be more motivated to succeed. It pushes me to think more creatively in terms of improving my situation. Though it's not always easy, it's important to keep moving forward," said Angela.

While new technologies have made it easier to launch independent ventures in the retail and service industries, they have also opened the way for entrepreneurs to re-imagine manufacturing and other parts of the economy. Many young people are using these advances to create sleek micro-multinationals with a global reach. Micro-multinationals are small companies with a presence in multiple countries. They also make more sense to Millennials, who grew up in a globalized world. Connecting with teams in Asia or Latin America on a project doesn't seem as big a hurdle when they've been signing onto chat rooms on the Internet since third grade. Micro-multinationals use online platforms such as Elance or RentaCoder to contract freelancers for marketing strategies or coding a website. They hire factories in China to produce goods on a small scale via Alibaba.com. These online-based services provide the resources of a big corporation at the fingertips of small operations, and for significantly lower overhead. In the post-crisis economy, new businesses have no choice but to streamline operations to unlock success. The only thing a person needs is a good idea.

Local Motors is one example. It is a radically new kind of car company, founded in Chandler, Arizona, by Jay Rogers, a former United States marine. Local Motors uses an online community of twelve thousand freelance designers from 121 countries and participate in contests and collectively design next-generation cars. The company then manufactures the winning cars using a network of microfactories.[3] In the end, more people are working, even if all the operations are smaller.

Dollar Shave Club is another one of those great ideas. Cofounded in 2012 by Michael Dubin, just 33 years old, the company offers a subscription plan and delivery service for basic razor blades for men's grooming. Shaving supplies are often expensive, and men have to remember to restock regularly. Dollar Shave Club supplies an answer to both those problems. Depending on the plan a customer chooses, the program costs just $3 to $9 a month, compared to fancy razors bought in a store that can cost more than $12 for the handle alone and $20 for a four-pack of refill cartridges. Dollar Shave Club can undercut the competition by cutting out the middleman—stores. It operates solely online. The company hired manufacturers in China and South Korea to make their blades cheaply.[4] The idea resonated with so many people that its promotional video on You-Tube had been viewed more than four million times just a couple of months after the company launched. In this über-connected world, Facebook, Twitter, and YouTube are just some of the ways promoting businesses has become a lot easier and cheaper. They allow companies to stay stream-lined, but offer them the world, literally, as an audience. Now Gen Yers can become their own public relations machine. When Dollar Shave Club made its first commercial, it didn't hire a spokesperson or model. Michael Dubin was the star of the commercial, because so often today business isn't just about the product; it's also about who is behind the product. Even Millennials who aren't entrepreneurs should follow this same manner of thinking. Since there is no clear career track in a company anymore, the only way to forge ahead is to think like your own small business within a company and be your own best advocate.

FLEXIBILITY

Successful Generation Y businesses are also focused on staying flexible. In this light, Shaun Walker's advertising agency is the perfectly modern post-crisis enterprise. It uti-lizes a flexible work model that includes prioritizing col-laboration with competitors over competition. In the end, everybody wins.

After graduating from the University of Southern Mis-sissippi in 2006 with a degree in advertising, Shaun found himself folding khakis and sweaters at a local Gap. It was the only job he could find. After five months of dogged hunting, he finally landed a job at one of New Orleans's largest advertising agencies. But after about two years, the financial market turned for the worse and Shaun got laid off. Not one for self-pity, Sean soon decided to start his own business. "It was the middle of the crisis, and we just decided if nobody was going to be able to offer us a job we were just going to make our own," said Shaun.

The advertising firm he cofounded with partner Reid Stone is called HERO|farm. A total marketing strategy and design agency, HERO|farm was named the 2011 Business of the Year in New Orleans, a distinction awarded by the International Association of Business Communicators. Why have Shaun and Reid been so successful? They have learned to be flexible. Shaun, who used to be a copywriter, can't afford to be a specialist anymore. He has picked up graphic design and other elements of advertising in order to trim costs. In addition, Shaun, Reid, and their one employee operate out of a makeshift office in Reid's apartment. They hire freelancers to fill in the gaps, and collaborate with other small firms on projects. By cooperating with other companies in the city, they build their brand and are able to earn money on other people's jobs, even though it's a smaller sum than they might have earned independently. They also do "ghost work" for larger firms. They give up recognition, but at least they are working in their field. Their salary is also unstable: "Right now, we don't have salaries per se," said Shaun. "Depending how much money is in the account, we'll sometimes make a little more, sometimes a little less. We always make sure to pay the employees first. It's scary at times—that's for sure. But it's definitely more rewarding," he said. "If you are going to put in tons of long hours, you may as well be doing it for yourself." Following this model for Millennials might also mean forgoing benefits and health care, since health care in America is tied to employers and is very costly, and often of low quality, when purchased independently.

Flexibility in the post-crisis economy extends beyond entrepreneurs. Career advisers say members of Generation Y should start thinking about jobs as more fluid and mobile, with inconsistent salaries making saving and long-term money planning all the more important. They should be open to changing careers, getting different types of training, and adjusting timing expectations for certain rites of passage, such as being able to afford to purchase a home. That could mean becoming more comfortable with accepting a role as one of the thousands of freelancers offering services cheaply on one of those new online contractor portals. That might also signal it's time to change your definition of being a grown-up, because stability is likely out the window. It could also include moving to a new place to call home, in order to find a new path for success, a different kind of good life.

Robin Canfield, 26, is a case in point. She graduated from one of the top international business schools in the country, Thunderbird School of Global Management, but it took her months to find a job with a decent salary. She had to make certain sacrifices. Rather than work in marketing, her area of focus, her new position is in public relations for luxury resorts and travel. Second, she had to pack her bags. Her new job required Robin to move more than 3,000 miles, from San Francisco to Miami.

"Previously, I was looking for a marketing job with a consumer products company out in California. Based on my experience and education, in a normal market this should have been easy," said Robin. But "these days, especially in my generation, you have to move where the opportunity is. Otherwise you're just setting yourself up for failure. I think in the current market, 20-somethings who lack the ten-plus years of experience of others have to do whatever it takes to find a job and success."

PROACTIVITY

Like Robin, Generation Y has to be more proactive to find success and plan for the future, since the present is so unstable. That means facing some terrifying realities, such as figuring out your investment and savings options for retirement and realizing that the government likely won't be able to help you as much as it supported previous generations. Millennials can also be proactive politically.

Generation Y has no real strong arm in Washington today, but that doesn't mean it couldn't. Young people helped put President Obama in office in 2008 with vocal public support and small online contributions that mounted into something meaningful. The drive turned Generation Y into a decisive voting bloc. As Generation Y ages, its significance in elections will only grow. By 2012, forty-six million young people will be eligible to vote.[5] Besides voting and campaigning, young people can take advantage of new PAC rules to influence the issues that matter most to our generation. Super PACs can raise unlimited sums of money from corporations, unions, associations, and individuals and can then use that money to advocate for or against candidates and the issues they stand for. To be sure, the freedom given to super PACs is another example of policy corrupting politics, but the policy is there. Stephen Colbert, host of *The Colbert Report* on Comedy Central, encouraged young people across college campuses to utilize super PACs during the 2012 election season, after launching his own, Americans for a Better Tomorrow, Tomorrow, to spotlight how corporations and lobby groups can use their very deep pockets to influence politics. Already, in a sign of just how influential these groups are, by the first half of 2012, 535 groups organized as super PACs reported total receipts of more than $200 million for the year, according to Open Secrets.org. This figure dwarfs the amount that PACs received in all of 2008, $40 million, before they became "super" and when there were limits on campaign spending. Eventually, more members of Generation Y will also have to emerge as politicians themselves to create new opportunities for new times. So far, this process has been slow, as the average age of legislators has been on the rise for some time, including new senators, who are typically over 50 years old.[6] A poll of more than three thousand Millennials between the ages of 18 and 29, conducted by the Harvard University Institute of Politics in the spring of 2012, hints at some of the reasons Generation Yers are put off by politics, despite their interest in work that can make a difference. Nearly 60 percent of survey respondents agree that elected officials seem to be motivated by selfish reasons; just about 30 percent find the idea of working in some form of public service appealing, which is about the same proportion as those who don't find it appealing and the same as those who don't care either way; nearly half of respondents feel that politics today is no longer able to meet the challenges the United States is facing. But becoming more politically proactive can help Generation Y build the kind of society its members want the United States to become.

What kind of future would Generation Y want to build in the United States, anyway? Surveys of emerging leaders hint at the answer. In a survey of more than a thousand young Americans participating in either the National Student Leadership Conference, courses with Americans for Informed Democracy, or a Washington, D.C., internship program, 38 percent identified as Democrat, 26 percent identified as Republican, and a significant 29 percent were independents.[7] Research shows that the high incidence of identification as independent may be a long-term phenomenon of U.S. politics into the future. Economists Paola Giuliano and Antonio Spilimbergo determined that when people grow up during a recession, the deeper and more sustained the crisis is, the less likely it is that these young citizens will identify with a party.[8] After all, their thinking likely goes, what did that party do for them? However, Giuliano and Spilimbergo's analysis of data collected annually since 1972 found that experiencing an economic recession between the ages of 18 and 25 compelled Americans to favor what might be considered more "leftist" governmental policies and higher taxes, even if they didn't identify with a political party. A Pew Research Center survey conducted in 2011 found the same: a majority of Millennials favored a greater level of federal spending to help the economy recover from the recession, rather than reducing the federal budget deficit. They also support federal efforts to reduce economic inequality.[9] Giuliano and Spilimbergo offer a reason this may be the case: a lack of confidence in themselves and government. "We find that individuals experiencing recessions during the formative years believe that luck rather than effort is the most important driver of individual success, support more government redistribution, and have less confidence in institutions," they write.

In other words, if the effects of this financial crisis

continue to burden Generation Y, young people stop believing in the American dream that hard work offers rewards. That could threaten the burgeoning success stories of these Millennials, and the future of this country. Generation Y may try to save itself today, but what about tomorrow?

Conclusion: The Future?

HOLLY: We are living in, like, the unluckiest time ever. I mean, I grew up
thinking I was born in the time when there was the Internet, and the fall
of communism, and the Gap. Turns out my time is when there's, like,
9/11 and a bunch of wars and the end of everything.

—*Six Feet Under*, Season 5, Episode 11

We now face a make-or-break moment for the middle class and those
trying to reach it. After decades of eroding middle-class security as those
at the very top saw their incomes rise as never before and after a historic
recession that plunged our economy into a crisis from which we are still
fighting to recover, it is time to construct an economy that is built to last.

—From **President Barack Obama's** proposed federal budget for fiscal year 2013

Generation Y has freedoms and technologies and advantages
that previous generations may have never even dreamed of.
As a result, the expectations are high for Millennials and
their future. In the American dream, hard work would get
us to where we want to go. Today, though, it's time to face
reality. And the financial crisis has thrown reality into our
faces at high speed.

In 2012, as President Obama geared up for his reelec-
tion campaign, he laid out a plan for the country's young
people. He said he would propose an increase in funds for
vocational training and employment in manufacturing;
an increase in federal funding for college loans and work-
study programs, to support low-income students; and put

more money into community colleges through a fund that would partner with businesses. He also proposed a number of programs to reeducate young people with the right skills for fields lacking enough workers. It is not enough, but it is something, and it is surely meaningful.

However, presidents don't always keep the promises they make during election years. Lobbyists, campaign contributors, and big businesses might hold leaders accountable for their own interests. For instance, people 50 years old and over have the powerful American Association of Retired Persons fighting for them. However, there is no strong organization in Washington, D.C., to represent Generation Y. We are not that organized yet. Nor do most members of Generation Y usually have enough expendable income to make significant campaign contributions that could influence politicians. And that makes Generation Y easy to ignore.

So, to President Obama as his second term in office takes off—or to the winners of subsequent presidential races—how about creating at least one reliable job for a member of Generation Y in 2013: a new Office for Youth? This agency would hold government accountable for its promises to our future. The office would report directly to the president on the issues most important to the country's younger generations, and respond to policies from the Labor Department, the Department of Education, and other relevant bodies. It would have the ability to initiate programs and request funding, and it would represent a group that has long been ignored by government. The position would be the voice of a generation and a conscience that the United States government is so clearly missing.

Besides calling on Congress and the president to follow through on their promises, the Office of Youth could also facilitate programming in communities across the United States by liaising with nonprofits and the private sector. The office's activities would be completely transparent, and it would publicly post its initiatives on a website, so citizens will know its objectives and members of government cannot ignore it—and, one hopes, will work to make its goals happen.

Key priorities should include:

- Creating desperately needed educational programs in classrooms across America on personal money management, loans, and financial planning for the future, and securing the support of city mayors to teach this curriculum in schools
- Educating about alternatives to four-year universities, and working with government, private groups, and schools to remove the stigma associated with those alternatives
- Building a pool of voluntary financial advisers to aid young people as they transition to independence
- Strengthening internship programs for high school students and ties with local businesses to help young people establish links to the workplace from an earlier age
- Encouraging more career guidance from a younger age
- Finding support for entrepreneurship education programs
- Raising money for more scholarships and creating more private-to-public grant matching programs
- Working with community programs and government departments to support more skills training, perhaps offered as subsidized after-school activities
- Planning World Economic Forum–like meetings with the world's top thinkers and leaders to put the spotlight

on youth and the future, with proceeds going toward the office's programs

- Building more incentives for parent involvement
- Holding events with young community leaders that facilitate direct communication with the president, in order to empower Generation Y to think creatively about its future and make tomorrow's leaders feel that they have a stake in this country's success
- Building volunteer programs that offer useful skills training and potential job networks and that could address other gaps in policy, such as health care services

Before a company or the government creates new positions, it usually undertakes a cost-benefit analysis. The analysis here is simple: regularly high unemployment for young people and a dearth of opportunities will result in lower economic growth in the United States, higher government costs for unemployment insurance, lost tax income, wasted productivity, brain drain, and elevated crime rates.

The good news is that Generation Y still believes we can all make a difference. It is a group that wants to offer the world more than it has received. Millennials are much more interested in public service than previous generations, and surveys by the Pew Research Center show confidence in their own ability, and the ability of government, to make a positive impact—even though they don't see that happening now. The Office of Youth, with the support of the next president, could ensure a better future for Generation Y and America.

ACKNOWLEDGMENTS

This book is the product of hundreds of conversations, thousands of hours of research, and a passion to tell Generation Y's story in the aftermath of the financial crisis, with the hope that something may change. I'm thankful to my colleagues at Dow Jones Newswires and the *Wall Street Journal* for allowing me the time to pursue this project. I'm also thankful to my agent, Rachel Sussman of Chalberg & Sussman, for the amount of time she spent perfecting my pitch and believing in this book. Thanks to Kathryn Whitenight, an exceptional and gracious editor, who even agreed to work on a four-month timeline.

Sections of this book could not have been completed without the reporting of Yuanni Chen in China and Michael Penn of the Shingetsu Institute in Japan, who conducted interviews with local residents.

I have the deepest gratitude to those who shared their personal stories with me, and those who helped connect me with friends and family to interview. Your honesty moved me, and I endeavored to translate our conversations onto these pages with accuracy and sensitivity. I am also appreciative of the publications, research institutes, and academics, listed in the endnotes, such as Demos and Brookings

Institution, which provided their expertise and data.

I also want to thank Esfira, Joseph, Polina, Jake, and Samson for their ideas, feedback, provocative questions, and happy distractions. Thank you for your support, Chuck, Risa, Sarah, and Ben. Love and thanks to Lee for his support, patience, inspiration, creativity, talent, and more patience.

ENDNOTES

PROLOGUE: THE AMERICAN DREAM

1. Adam Dickter, "NYANA To Close After Long Run Here," *The Jewish Week*, June 25, 2008.

INTRODUCTION: THE END OF THE GOOD LIFE

1. Bureau of Labor Statistics.
2. Meta Brown, Andrew Haughwout, Donghoon Lee, Maricar Mabutas, and Wilbert van der Klaauw, "Grading Student Loans," *Liberty Street Economics,* Federal Reserve Bank of New York, March 5, 2012, http://libertystreeteconomics.newyork fed.org/2012/03/grading-student-loans.html.
3. Sewell Chan, "Crisis Panel's Report Parsed Far and Wide," *New York Times*, January 27, 2011.
4. The Congress of the United States Congressional Budget Office, "The Budget and Economic Outlook: Fiscal Years 2011 to 2021," January 2011.
5. Frank Levy and Peter Temin, "Inequality and Institutions in 20th Century America," Massachusetts Institute of Technology Working Paper Series, June 27, 2007.
6. John Schmitt, "Inequality as Policy: The United States Since 1979," Center for Economic and Policy Research, October 2009.
7. Richard Fry, D'Vera Cohn, Gretchen Livingston, and Paul Taylor, "The Rising Age Gap in Economic Well-Being," Pew Research Center, November 7, 2011.

8. Gregory Acs, "Downward Mobility from the Middle Class: Waking Up from the American Dream," Pew Charitable Trusts, September 6, 2011.

9. "Trends in the Distribution of Household Income Between 1979 and 2007," Congressional Budget Office, October 25, 2011.

10. John E. Silvia, Tim Quinlan, and Joe Seydl, "Economic Mobility: Is 'Rags to Riches' Still Possible?" Wells Fargo, November 15, 2011.

11. Economic Policy Institute.

12. Jason DeParle, "Harder for Americans to Rise From Lower Rungs," *New York Times*, January 4, 2012; Kate Pickett and Richard Wilkinson, *The Spirit Level: Why Equality Is Better for Everyone* (London: Penguin, 2010).

13. Joseph Stiglitz, "Of the 1 Percent, by the 1 Percent, for the 1 Percent," *Vanity Fair*, May 2011.

14. Richard Wilkinson, "How Economic Inequality Harms Societies," TED, July 2011, www.ted.com/talks/richard_wilkinson.html.

1: THIS NEW AMERICAN LIFE: GENERATION Y AND THE GREAT RECESSION

1. "The State of Young America: The Poll," Demos and Young Invincibles, November 2011.

2. Richard Fry, D'Vera Cohn, Gretchen Livingston, and Paul Taylor, "The Rising Age Gap in Economic Well-Being," Pew Research Center, November 7, 2011.

3. Daniel Sullivan and Till von Wachter, "Job Displacement and Mortality: An Analysis Using Administrative Data," *Quarterly Journal of Economics*, August 2009.

4. "The Jobless Young," *Economist*, September 10, 2011.

5. Lisa Kahn, "The Long-Term Labor Market Consequences of Graduating from College in a Bad Economy," Yale School of Management, August 13, 2009.

6. Dennis Cauchon, "Household Electricity Bills Skyrocket," *USA Today*, December 13, 2011.

7. "The State of Young America: The Databook," Demos and Young Invincibles, November 2011.

8. "Educational Attainment in the United States: 2011," United States Census Bureau.

9. "Student Loan Debt Clock," FinAid, www.finaid.org/loans/studentloandebtclock.phtml.

10. "Survey: 4 out of 5 U.S. Bankruptcy Attorneys Report Major Jump in Student Loan Debtors Seeking Help, Fears Grow of Next Mortgage-Style Debt Threat to U.S.," National Association of Consumer Bankruptcy Attorneys, February 7, 2012.

11. United States Census Bureau.

12. Leslie Kwoh, "Asia's Endangered Species: The Expat," *Wall Street Journal*, March 28, 2012.

13. "Survey: 4 out of 5 U.S. Bankruptcy Attorneys Report Major Jump."

14. Kelly Field, "Government Vastly Undercounts Defaults," *Chronicle of Higher Education*, July 11, 2010, http://chronicle.com/article/Many-More-Students-Are/66223.

15. John Quinterno and Viany Orozco, "The Great Cost Shift: How Higher Education Cuts Undermine the Future Middle Class," Demos, April 2012.

16. Andrew Manshel, "Why Top Colleges Squeeze You Dry," *Wall Street Journal*, April 7, 2010.

17. Nate Johnson, "What Does a College Degree Cost?," Delta Cost Project White Paper Series, March 2009.

18. "The State of Young America: The Poll," Demos and Young Invincibles, November 2011.

19. Rakesh Kochhar and D'Vera Cohn, "Fighting Poverty in a Bad Economy, Americans Move In with Relatives," Pew Research Center, October 3, 2011.

20. Jesse Bricker, Arthur B. Kennickell, Kevin B. Moore, and John Sabelhaus, "Changes in U.S. Family Finances from 2007 to 2010: Evidence from the Survey of Consumer Finances," *Federal Reserve Bulletin*, June 2012.

21. "The State of Young America: The Databook," Demos and Young Invincibles, November 2011.

22. S&P/Case-Shiller Home Price Indices 2010–2012.

23. Ben Bernanke, "The Coming Demographic Transition: Will We Treat Future Generations Fairly?," presented at the Washington Economic Club, Washington, D.C., October 4, 2006.

24. Linda A. Jacobsen, Mary Kent, Marlene Lee, and Mark Mather, "America's Aging Population," *Population Reference Bureau Population Bulletin* 66, no. 1 (February 2011).

25. Alex Blumberg and Andrea Seabrook, "461: Take the Money and Run for Office," *This American Life*, March 30, 2012.

2: EUROPE IN CRISIS

1. Laurence Ball, Daniel Leigh, and Prakash Loungani, "Painful Medicine," *Finance & Development* 48, no. 3 (September 2011).

2. Amartya Sen, "Austerity Is Undermining Europe's Grand Vision," *Guardian*, July 3, 2012.

3. Robert E. Lucas Jr., "Macroeconomic Priorities," speech to the American Economic Association, January 10, 2003.

4. Ben S. Bernanke, "The Great Moderation," speech to the Eastern Economic Association, Washington, D.C., February 20, 2004.

5. David Fergusson, L. John Horwood, and Lianne Woodward, "Unemployment and Psychosocial Adjustment in Young Adults: Causation or Selection?" *Social Science and Medicine* 53, no. 3 (August 2001); Fiona Carmichael and Robert Ward, "Youth Unemployment and Crime in the English Regions and Wales," *Applied Economics* 32 (2000).

6. "Education at a Glance 2011," Organisation for Economic Co-operation and Development.

7. "OECD (2010)—Off to a Good Start? Jobs for Youth United Kingdom," Organisation for Economic Cooperation and Development, December 15, 2010.

8. "Average UK Student Debts 'Could Hit £53,000," BBC, August 11, 2011.

9. "Migration Statistics and Labour Force Survey," Eurostat, 2010.

10. David N. F. Bell and David G. Blanchflower, "Youth Unemployment: Déjà Vu?" University of Stirling, November 27, 2009.

3: BREAKING IT DOWN: THE LABOR MARKET IS RIGGED
AGAINST GENERATION Y

1. David H. Autor and Susan N. Houseman, "Do Temporary-Help Jobs Improve Labor Market Outcomes for Low-Skilled

Workers? Evidence from 'Work First,'" *American Economic Journal: Applied Economics*, July 2010.

2. Richard Dobbs, James Manyika, and Charles Roxburgh, "What Business Can Do to Restart Growth," McKinsey & Company, September 2011.

3. "Corporate Profits After Tax," Federal Reserve Bank of St. Louis, June 28, 2012, http://research.stlouisfed.org/fred2/series /CP.

4. Nir Jaimovich and Henry E. Siu, "The Trend Is the Cycle: Job Polarization and Jobless Recoveries," March 31, 2012; Mike Dorning, "Obama Fails to Stem Middle-Class Slide He Blamed on Bush," *Bloomberg,* May 1, 2012.

5. James Manyika, Susan Lund, Byron Auguste, Lenny Mendonca, Tim Welsh, and Sreenivas Ramaswamy, "An Economy That Works: Job Creation and America's Future," McKinsey & Company, June 2011.

6. John Evans and Euan Gibb, "Moving from Precarious Employment to Decent Work," Global Union Research Network, 2009.

7. "Improved Outreach Could Help Ensure Proper Worker Classification," Government Accountability Office, 2006.

8. Francesca Dota, "International Patterns of Precarious Work Among Young People," presented at the seminar "Young People and Precarious Work," ESRC Seminar Series, Coventry University, March 11, 2011.

9. Francesca Dota, "Economic Crisis and Flexibility in Italy: The 'Tsunami' of Youth Unemployment," presented at the seminar "Young People and Precarious Work," ESRC Seminar Series, Coventry University, March 11, 2011.

10. Alfonso Rosolia and Roberto Torrini, "The Generation Gap: An Analysis of the Decline of Relative Wages of Young Italian Males," 2006.

11. Italian National Institute of Statistics.

12. Eurostat, "Europe 2020 Indicators Education: Tertiary educational attainment by sex, age group 30–34," 2011.

13. National Institute for Statistics, 2011.

14. "Employment Measures for Young People," Japan Ministry of Health, Labour, and Welfare, March 8, 2011.

15. Martin Fackler, "In Japan, Young Face Generational Road-blocks," *New York Times*, January 27, 2011.
16. Chad Steinberg and Masato Nakane, "To Fire or to Hoard? Explaining Japan's Labor Market Response in the Great Recession," IMF Working Paper, January 2011.
17. Toshi Nakamura, "Japan's Newest RPG Hero Is Unemployed," *Kotaku*, March 8, 2012.
18. Yuji Genda, "Who Really Lost Jobs in Japan? Youth Employment in an Aging Japanese Society," National Bureau of Economic Research, January 2003.
19. "Employment Projections: 2010–2020 Summary," *Bureau of Labor Statistics*, February 1, 2012.

4: EXPECTATIONS CRUSHED, YOUNG LEAVE IRELAND: A WARNING AS UNITED STATES BRAIN DRAIN RISK MOUNTS

1. Alan Barrett, Ide Kearney, Thomas Conefrey, and Cormac O'Sullivan, "Quarterly Economic Commentary, Winter 2010," The Economic and Social Research Institute, January 2011.
2. Stuart Anderson and Michael Platzer, "American Made: The Impact of Immigrant Entrepreneurs and Professionals on U.S. Competitiveness," National Venture Capital Association, 2006.
3. Vivek Wadhwa, Guillermina Jasso, Ben Rissing, Gary Gereffi, and Richard Freeman, "Intellectual Property, the Immigration Backlog, and a Reverse Brain-Drain," August 2007.
4. Subra Suresh, "Public Comments to the President's Council of Advisors on Science and Technology," January 7, 2011.

5: THE VIEW FROM THE NEW PROMISED LANDS

1. Charles Duhigg and Keith Bradsher, "How the U.S. Lost Out on iPhone Work," *New York Times*, January 21, 2012.
2. "National Economic Confidence," Ipsos, February 2012.
3. "Tracking Global Trends: New Study Identifies Six Key Developments Shaping the Business World," Ernst & Young, March 29, 2011.
4. "Science and Engineering Indicators 2012," National Science Board, January 2012.

5. Peter L. Meyer, "Brazil-U.S. Relations," Congressional Research Service, February 9, 2011.

6. Homi Kharas, "The Emerging Middle Class in Developing Countries," Organization for Economic Cooperation and Development, January 2010.

7. Jeffrey Passel, D'Vera Cohn, and Ana Gonzalez-Barrera, "Net Migration from Mexico Falls to Zero—and Perhaps Less," Pew Hispanic Center, April 23, 2012.

8. "Statement at the Conclusion of the IMF and World Bank Financial Sector Assessment Program Mission to Brazil," International Monetary Fund, March 21, 2012.

9. Silvio Cascione and Todd Benson, "Mantega: Brazil Accelerating Despite Global Slump," *Reuters*, May 28, 2012.

10. Institute of International Finance, Inc.

11. Cristiane Lucchesi, "Pay Jumps 25 Percent for Brazilian Investment Bankers Ready to Defect," *Bloomberg*, January 18, 2012.

12. "Ease of Doing Business in Brazil," World Bank, http://www.doingbusiness.org/data/exploreeconomies/brazil/#starting-a-business.

13. "Hurun Wealth Report 2011," Bank of China and *Hurun Report*, 2011.

6: BATTLE FOR GENERATION Y'S FUTURE: AMERICA'S DEFICIT VERSUS GROWTH

1. Mark Thoma, "The Destructive, Ideological Push for Austerity," *Economist's View*, June 27, 2012.

2. "How the Across-the-Board Cuts in the Budget Control Act Will Work," Richard Kogan, Center on Budget and Policy Priorities, April 27, 2012.

3. Brad Plumer, "What Paul Ryan's budget actually cuts—and by how much," *Washington Post*, Ezra's Wonk Blog, March 20, 2012; Howard Gleckman, "Paul Ryan's Budget Plan: More Big Tax Cuts for the Rich," Tax Policy Center, Urban Institute and Brookings Institution, March 23, 2012; Paul Ryan, "Path to Prosperity: A Blueprint For American Renewal," March 20, 2012.

4. "Bank for International Settlements 82nd Annual Report," Bank for International Settlements, June 24, 2012.

5. Damian Paletta, "S&P Official: U.S. Downgrade Was Due in Part to Debt-Ceiling Brawl," *Wall Street Journal*, August 5, 2011.

6. "Economists to Governor: Raise High-End Income Taxes to Help Close Budget Gaps," Fiscal Policy Institute, December 2008.

7. Kevin G. Hall and Robert A. Rankin, "What Should We Do About National Debt, and When?," McClatchy Newspapers, August 17, 2010.

8. "The Budget and Economic Outlook: Fiscal Years 2012 to 2022," Congressional Budget Office, January 31, 2012.

9. Warren E. Buffett, "Stop Coddling the Super-Rich," *New York Times*, August 14, 2011.

7: THE RIGHT BUDGET CHOICES: FROM EDUCATION TO THE WORKPLACE

1. "Not Just for the Elite: A History of College Student Loans in America," Random History, 2008.

2. Elizabeth Warren, Sandy Baum, and Ganesh Sitaraman, "Service Pays: Creating Opportunities by Linking College with Public Service," *Harvard Law and Policy Review* 127 (2007).

3. P. W. Singer, Heather Messera, and Brendan Orino, "What Does the Next Generation of American Leaders Think?," Brookings Institution, February 2011.

4. Kelly Field, "Student Lenders, Fighting to Survive, Spend Millions to Lobby Congress," *Chronicle of Higher Education*, September 28, 2009.

5. "Undercover Testing Finds Colleges Encouraged Fraud and Engaged in Deceptive and Questionable Marketing Practices," U.S. Government Accountability Office, August 4, 2010.

6. Catherine Rampell, "Out of Community Colleges and into For-Profits," *New York Times*, March 5, 2012.

7. *Where We Stand. America's Schools in the 21st Century*, PBS, 2008; Margaret Spellings, "Maintaining the Federal Role in Accountability," *Education Week*, January 9, 2012.

8. Sean F. Reardon, "The Widening Academic Achievement Gap Between the Rich and the Poor: New Evidence and Possible

Explanations," in *Whither Opportunity? Rising Inequality and the Uncertain Life Chances of Low-Income Children*, ed. R. Murnane and G. Duncan (New York: Russell Sage Foundation Press, 2011).

9. "Strong Performers and Successful Reformers in Education: Lessons from PISA for the United States," Organization for Economic Cooperation and Development, 2011.

10. W. Norton Grubb, "Dynamic Inequality and Intervention: Lessons from a Small Country," *Phi Delta Kappan* 89, 2 (Oct. 2007).

11. Alan Blinder, "Alan Blinder: Stimulus Isn't a Dirty Word," *Wall Street Journal*, June 25, 2012.

12. "Report of the President's Commission to Study Capital Budgeting," February 1999.

13. Emilia Istrate and Robert Puentes, "Investing for Success: Examining a Federal Capital Budget and a National Infrastructure Bank," Brookings Institution, December 2009.

14. "Capital Budgeting," Congressional Budget Office, May 2008.

15. Alec Ian Gershberg and Joseph Benning, "Federal Capital Investment and the Balanced Budget Amendment: the Pros and Cons of a Federal Capital Budget," Nelson A. Rockefeller Institute of Government, December 1999.

16. "Pathways to Prosperity: Meeting the Challenge of Preparing Young Americans for the 21st Century," Harvard Graduate School of Education, February 2011.

17. "Report Calls for National Effort to Get Millions of Young American onto a Realistic Path to Employability," Harvard Graduate School of Education, February 2, 2011.

18. Harry J. Holzer, "Testimony Before the Budget Committee of the United States Senate," September 2011.

19. James Haltiwanger, Ron Jarmin, and Javier Miranda, "Historically Large Decline in Job Creation from Startup and Existing Firms in the 2008–2009 Recession," Ewing Marion Kauffman Foundation, March 2011.

20. Demetrios G. Papademetriou and Madeleine Sumption, "The Role of Immigration in Fostering Competitiveness in the United States," Migration Policy Institute, May 2011; Demetrios G. Papademetriou, Doris Meissner, Marc R. Rosenblum, and Madeleine Sumption, "Aligning Temporary Immigration Visas

with U.S. Labor Market Needs: The Case for a New System of Provisional Visas," Migration Policy Institute, July 2009.

21. "Women Can't Afford Unfair Pay Today," National Women's Law Center, April 2012.

22. Janet G. Stotsky, "Gender and Its Relevance to Macroeconomic Policy: A Survey," International Monetary Fund, October 2006.

23. "How a Competitiveness Audit Can Help Create Jobs," Progressive Policy Institute, November 2011.

8: HOW GENERATION Y CAN SAVE ITSELF

1. Nick Shore, "Turning on the 'No Collar' Workforce," *In Media Daily News,* March 15, 2012.

2. "Internet Matters: The Net's Sweeping Impact on Growth, Jobs, and Prosperity," McKinsey Global Institute, May 2011.

3. Ann Mettler and Anthony D. Williams, "The Rise of the Micro-Multinational: How Freelancers and Technology-Savvy Start-Ups Are Driving Growth, Jobs and Innovation," Lisbon Council Policy Brief, October 2011.

4. Emily Glazer, "A David and Gillette Story," *Wall Street Journal,* April 12, 2012.

5. "Youth Demographics," Center for Information and Research on Civic Learning and Engagement, www.civicyouth.org/quick-facts/youth-demographics.

6. Jonathan Bernstein, "Where Are the Young Pols?" *Salon,* May 19, 2012.

7. P. W. Singer, Heather Messera, and Brendan Orino, "What Does the Next Generation of American Leaders Think?," Brookings Institution, February 2011.

8. Paola Giuliano and Antonio Spilimbergo, "Growing Up in a Recession: Beliefs and the Macroeconomy," National Bureau of Economic Research, September 2009.

9. Morley Winograd and Michael D. Hais, "Will Millennials Still Be Liberal When They're Old and Gray?" *New Geography,* March 1, 2012; "Angry Silents, Disengaged Millennials. The Generation Gap and the 2012 Election," Pew Research Center, November 3, 2011.

INDEX

unemployment
current rates of, 9, 32
in the European Union (EU),
50–53, 55, 58–64, 69, 73–74
in the U.S., 9, 11, 22–23, 25,
27–28, 32, 39–40
United Arab Emirates, 51
United Kingdom, 9–10, 18, 55,
73–78, 123, 184
United States. *See also* American Dream; education
reform
austerity programs, 55,
144–160
brain drain in, 113–121
credit rating downgrade, 146,
151
culture of innovation, 18–19.
See also entrepreneurs
deficit versus economic
growth policies, 13,
144–160
economic mobility in, 17–18
economic policies of, 11–15
education reforms, 161–177
End of the Good Life and,
6–8, 201–204
federal budget reforms to
support education, 174–177
government funding for education, 15–16
Great Recession of 2008 and
2009, 6, 9, 12, 19–20, 53–54
improving competitiveness,
183–188
income gap in, 14–15, 16–18
Irish economy lessons,
113–121

Japanese economy lessons,
95–100
labor market in. *See* labor
market
Office for Youth (proposed),
202–204
opportunity gap in, 36–37
protest movements. *See* protest movements
tax policy. *See* tax policy,
U.S.
U.S. Bureau of Labor Statistics,
33, 81, 85–86, 187–188
U.S. Congressional Budget Office, 12, 154, 157, 177
U.S. Department of Education,
171, 202
U.S. Department of Homeland
Security, 119
U.S. Department of Labor, 202
U.S. Department of State,
113–114
U.S. Government Accountability Office, 87
University of California, 163–164
University of Phoenix, 170–171
Upstart, 164–165
Urban Institute, 45–46

Vassanelli, Marta, 90
Vatican Radio, 95
Vietnam, 32
visa rules, 184–185
volunteer programs, 147–148

Wachovia, 24
Walker, Shaun, 194–195
Walmart, 32

JOURNALIST RIVA FROYMOVICH has covered Europe's economy in the throes of collapse, the U.S. dollar's historic decline during the Great Recession, the rapid rise of emerging economies, central banks as they faced their biggest challenge since the Great Depression, and politicians' attempt to cobble together financial regulation. She has experience reporting in print and on camera for *The Wall Street Journal* and *Dow Jones Newswires*, among other outlets, after graduating cum laude from the New York University College of Arts & Science with a Bachelor of Arts in Journalism. She has appeared on Fox Business News, BBC, Sky Television, and the *Wall Street Journal*'s online video network. Riva is a member of Generation Y and calls New York home.